CAUGHT!

CAUGHT!

NABBING HISTORY'S MOST WANTED

GEORGIA BRAGG

Illustrated by KEVIN O'MALLEY

Crown Books for Young Readers
New York

For my brother, Charles Lynn Bragg

Text copyright © 2019 by Georgia Bragg
Jacket art and interior illustrations copyright © 2019 by Kevin O'Malley

Visit us on the Web! rhcbooks.com

Educators and librarians, for a variety of teaching tools, visit us at RHTeachersLibrarians.com

Library of Congress Cataloging-in-Publication Data is available upon request.
ISBN 978-1-5247-6741-9 (trade) — ISBN 978-1-5247-6742-6 (lib. bdg.) — ISBN 978-1-5247-6743-3 (ebook)

Printed in the United States of America
10 9 8 7 6 5 4 3 2 1
First Edition

Random House Children's Books supports the First Amendment
and celebrates the right to read.

CONTENTS

INTRODUCTION

Either Way, They're All Famous

Everyone in this book got caught for doing something; most were guilty, some were not. A handful had trials, others were hunted down, and a few were framed. A large number had second chances that they didn't take.

Whether cheating on a test or plotting to kidnap the president, no one likes to get caught. Billy the Kid, Blackbeard the Pirate, and everyone else in this book line up to a unique time in history. As Robert Kennedy said, "Every society gets the kind of criminal it deserves." There would be no Al Capone without Prohibition, no Anastasia impostor without the Russian Revolution, and no Joan of Arc without the Inquisition, because you can be sure if Joan of Arc lived today, no one would accuse her of being a witch. The times made the people, and the people made history.

This group of characters was more likely to murder, cheat, and hoard prize money than do good, but whatever they did, it put them on the map. In some way or another, they sparked the imagination and broke free of the pack with their catchy names and noteworthy deeds.

Gangsters, con artists, thieves, spies, and assassins—whether they were a force of change, entrapped by the narrow-minded, or just in the wrong place at the wrong time, they were all caught. Why read about these folks since their stories are unlikely to turn up on a school test? Because they changed history and made the world not only a more fascinating place, but a place that requires criminal forensics, mug shots, fingerprinting, ballistics, and DNA testing.

Caught! is full of history you can almost use.

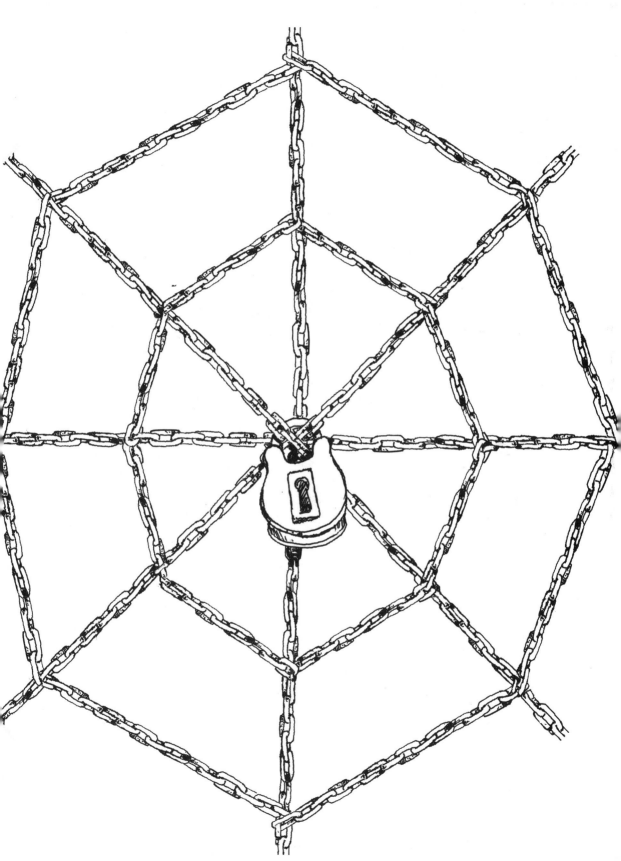

JOAN OF ARC

CERTIFIABLY JOAN

Born: c. 1412
Domrémy, France
Died: May 30, 1431
Rouen, France
19 years old

Joan of Arc is like the kind of friend you can't stand, but when you need her for something important, she's there at the rescue. It just so happened that when Joan was alive, France needed to be saved from invaders. She showed up and led the French army when she was only seventeen years old, at a time when girls were barely allowed to do more than peek out a tower window or feed a goat. Joan seemed like a regular teenager until she started hearing voices in her head. She believed she heard angels telling her to "rescue France." So she did. But when Joan was caught by the enemy and burned at the stake, nobody came to her rescue.

Joan was believed to have been born in 1412; this was the Middle Ages, which meant that there wasn't so much as a book, a toilet, or a lightbulb. Castles had moats, and the Catholic religion controlled everything. Joan lived next door to a church. Her reaction to the ding-donging church bell was the first indication Joan had a problem with self-control. A late-ringing church bell was enough to ruin her day, so she'd yell at the bell ringer if he rang the bell just a few minutes behind schedule. Praying was her favorite pastime, and even the priest thought Joan came to confession too often. Especially since her only sin was sneaking into the woods to be alone. Otherwise, like all peasant girls, Joan was put to work hoeing, fetching, and plucking, which she'd be expected to do without any chance of advancement until the day she died. At thirteen, when Joan started hearing voices no one else heard, she dropped her friends and became a loner—because the voices in her head were company enough. After two years, Joan finally understood what the voices were getting at: they wanted her to save France.

France needed all the help it could get. Besides plagues and famines, France had endured England's invasions for seventy-five years. Charles VII, the French king, hadn't been officially crowned, because the English king Henry VI had claimed the throne. The French believed God was punishing them, but they also believed the prediction (prophecy) that they'd be saved by a maiden, the old-maid kind—as in no boyfriends, ever.

Knowing the position was up for grabs, Joan started calling herself Joan the Maid. Then Joan needed to travel twelve miles to present herself to the French military leaders, but girls couldn't traipse off alone. Joan pestered an uncle to take her to a French captain, and she told the captain that God had given her two tasks: run the English out of the city of Orléans, and get France's un-crowned king crowned already.

But Joan's fulfilling her mission was as unlikely as a girl today playing quarterback at the Super Bowl. The only reason anyone would even consider such a tall order from a sixteen-year-old girl was that everyone lived and dreamed in superstitions, and they all believed the maiden prophecy was an actual thing.

Before they would listen to her, though, religious leaders tested Joan to make sure she was the maiden they'd been waiting for. "What language do your voices speak?"

"A better tongue than you do."

"Were they all of the same appearance?"

"Some had wings or were crowned."

Good enough.

When she went to meet Charles, her would-be king, everyone expected Joan to dress up and look pretty, but she put on men's clothes and got a man's haircut instead. That kind of gender-bending attire could get a person killed back then. Churchmen tried to exorcise the evil spirits they thought were inside her, but she still wouldn't change her clothes.

Charles thought Joan's ideas about how she'd win the war were a little screwy, but she was a breath of fresh air compared to the gloomy, defeated people he knew. So he granted Joan his royal A-OK to save France.

She was given a big white horse, armor, chain mail, shin plates, and a crash course in knight skills. She also got five swords, even though she wasn't expected to use those because no prophecied maid should be fighting. Instead, she'd be holding her new twelve-foot-long banner with angels emblazoned on it, announcing, "I'm on God's team."

She had a lot of nerve doing that. Concerned by the banner, Church officials wanted to know, "At whose direction did you have it painted in this fashion?"

"I have done nothing except at God's command. And I have told you this often enough." In short, *I've got this.*

Joan was raring to go. Recruitment numbers were way up, as men wanted to fight alongside God's appointed one. She took off with a few military captains and 2,500 bearded and burly men who'd grabbed something pointy (hammers, axes, pitchforks) to join the fight. Joan sent the English a written warning: *"I will drive them out; if they will not obey, I will put them all to death."*

The English believed in prophecies too; they were spooked.

When Joan rode into Orléans, a mob of her fans clamored to touch her. Meanwhile, the captains made battle plans, which made Joan angry because she thought she was in charge—and she wanted to attack immediately.

While she endured the delay, the city threw a parade in her honor, and she wrote the enemy again, basically saying, *Hey. Me again. I'm coming to kill you.*

Finally, she galloped off to her first battle, and she held her banner high for the three hours of hand-to-hand combat. Her presence inspired her soldiers to victory.

She wanted to attack other Orléans strongholds immediately, but the captains decided otherwise.

"You have been to your council, and I to mine," she argued. "And believe me, the counsel of my Lord will be put into effect. . . ." In other words, *Get out of my way.*

The soldiers liked her bloodthirsty impatience, now that they had won a battle, so the captains had to follow Joan into more battles, or they'd be left behind. That day ended up being one of the bloodiest in the Hundred Years' War. Forget sleeping; Joan was amped up and didn't stop fighting until she recaptured the whole city of Orléans.

After Mission One was a success, Joan's army grew to six thousand men, and they ran the English out of many more towns.

Joan got Charles crowned in 1429, according to her instructions. But she hadn't been instructed to upstage members of the court and the archbishop, nor to hog Charles's spotlight by waving her supersized banner during his coronation. Not to mention she was still dressed like a man.

Mission Two accomplished—she was golden. But it was quitting time. She had handled everything the angels told her to do, and they didn't have any new assignments for her. Neither did King

Charles VII, because the newly crowned French king was busy nego-tiating temporary cease-fire agreements with the English.

But Joan had no intention of going home, because the English were still in her country. "No matter how many truces are made like this, I am not at all happy. . . ." Joan had her heart set on taking back Paris when the truce ended, but Charles told her no, because he knew she'd get clobbered. Joan kept hammering away at Charles until he finally said okay.

Joan was so excited, she charged ahead without checking the cal-endar. She attacked on a religious holiday. No one ever did that, and it was a major no-no. Also, Joan was wounded when a six-inch cross-bow bolt pierced her leg. Her gung-ho, let's-get-Paris-back campaign was a failure.

The defeat, her injury, and the calendar snafu were obvious signs that God had abandoned her. The maiden prophecy was over. Joan's French followers dumped her.

King Charles told her, *Hey, thanks for everything; I've made you and your family nobility; please go home now.*

Joan didn't get the hint. She wouldn't listen to anyone, so without religious orders or divine guidance, Joan just did her own thing. Now, with only 400 men left from her 8,500-man army, Joan galloped out the main gate of the town of Compiègne and led the soldiers over the bridge to join in a skirmish. Her men begged her to stop because they were obviously outnumbered. It was a suicide mission.

"You be quiet!" she hollered. "Think only of striking at them."

Even though she was against it, her men hustled her back to the bridge. All Joan had to do was ride through the gates to safety, but she wouldn't do it. A few loyal soldiers stayed with her, but the rest of her men took off without her. The bridge was raised and the gate was shut with Joan still outside. She was pulled off her horse and captured by the English.

Not only was Joan the enemy, but the English believed her success had nothing to do with God at all. Her inspiration came from Satan.

Joan was locked in a tower, six or seven stories high. She assumed that King Charles was negotiating for her release, except he wasn't. Her voices told her to stay put, but being cooped up made Joan nutty enough to squirm out the tiny window to escape by jumping seventy feet into the castle's dry moat. The fall practically killed her. She didn't talk, move, or eat for days, but she lived.

Did she think she could fly? Was she trying to kill herself? Besides heresy, attempted suicide was now added to the list of un-Catholic activities that she'd have to answer for.

She went from rock star to being a rock target. Now almost everyone on both sides believed she was a witch. They locked her in wrist and leg irons so she couldn't jump out any more windows. While in bed, her irons were attached to a large block at the foot of the bed and three guards were locked in the cell with her.

Then they took her on a six-week trip through enemy territory to Rouen, the location of her trial with the Church police, known as the Inquisition.

She hadn't changed her clothes for the last nine months because God didn't tell her to, so when she met the sixty men who would decide her fate, she wasn't looking her best. She was offered a dress, but she refused to put it on.

Her months on trial were filled with hairsplitting details of everything the judges didn't like about Joan. She was charged with heresy and witchcraft, both punishable by death.

Not wanting to die, Joan signed a pledge that she would never again dress like a man, cut her hair short, or hold a weapon.

In her cell, she immediately put on a dress. But her freedom didn't come as quickly. While awaiting her release, a man came to her cell and tried to force himself on her. So three days later, Joan broke her pledge and put men's clothing back on because they were the only means of protection available to her.

The men's clothes may have kept her safe from attack, but they ultimately led to her untimely death, giving the English Inquisitors the only justification they needed to get rid of her. Pierre Cauchon, bishop of Beauvais, announced, "It is done."

That very day, May 30, 1431, an enormous crowd watched as Joan was burned alive at the stake, and burned again down to ashes, making doubly sure she was dead.

She was only nineteen years old when she died. The English thought Joan's story would be forgotten, but she is forever connected with the history of France. She was bold and she was different, but that was no reason to kill her. As a woman, sometimes you have to be very bold to break the mold. She was brave and bewitching, irritating and underappreciated during her brief lifetime. She did change the course of the Hundred Years' War when she was only a teenager, though she had to wait another four hundred years before finally earning the title of Saint Joan.

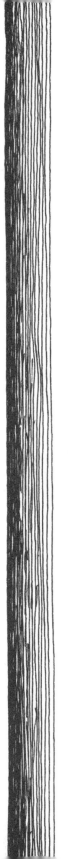

JOAN OF ARC FACTS AND STATS

JOAN DID NOT COME FROM A LAND CALLED ARC.
She was born in a town called Domrémy. Her dad's last name was d'Arc.

1 STRAND OF JOAN'S HAIR was found in the wax seal of one of her dictated letters. Joan of Arc had black hair, contrary to practically every painting depicting her. The single strand of hair disappeared sometime during the 1800s.

Unmarried girls wore their hair long and loose, signaling that they were single and available. But not Joan; she cut her hair short in a style still known in France today as *la coupe à la Jeanne d'Arc*.

3 SIGNATURES of Joan's have survived. Because she was illiterate, someone else wrote her letters for her and then she signed them with an X, until she eventually learned how to write her name.

9 OF JOAN'S DICTATED LETTERS STILL EXIST. Handwriting experts analyzed Joan's signature and concluded Joan was left-handed. In the Middle Ages, lefties were sometimes accused of witchcraft.

3 LOYAL SOLDIERS WERE CAPTURED with Joan. They were the only ones who stayed with her while the rest of her army fled. They were prisoners with Joan for a while, but they were eventually released.

Their Names and Identities:
- Pierre d'Arc: Joan's brother
- Jean d'Aulon: Joan's squire
- Jean d'Aulon's brother: Name unknown

2 LAYERS OF WOOLEN TIGHTS were tied together with cords to a tight coat (doublet) of Joan's male clothing. The outside layer had dozens of cords connecting both layers to her doublet. The inside layer had 20 more cords looping through eyelets, which was twice the norm, but Joan liked it because it protected her against the advances of men. It was also extremely hard to take a bathroom break.

40 TO 50 POUNDS was about the weight of Joan's armor. Joan never fought in a battle or killed anyone.

70 CHARGES were originally brought up against Joan.

12 CHARGES were finally brought against her in court.

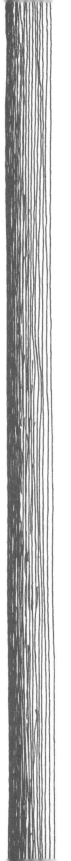

25 YEARS after her trial, Joan was declared innocent.

BY 1456 Joan had become a national heroine. The charges against her were wrong and her trial was ruled invalid. And the Church acknowledged that she had been "put to death very cruelly, iniquitously, and against reason."

464 YEARS LATER, in 1920, Joan was canonized by the Catholic Church for miraculously saving France, and several times healing the sick. She is now known as Saint Joan.

2 TIMES Joan was wounded in battle. Once she was shot in the shoulder by an arrow, and another time she was shot in the thigh with a crossbow bolt.

 Joan's ashes were thrown in the Seine River.

MIDDLE AGES TREASURY OF WORDS

- **Heresy:** an opinion contrary to Church beliefs
- **Heretic:** a person who believes something different from the Catholic Church
- **Hundred Years' War:** arising out of English kings claiming the French crown from 1337 to 1453
- **Inquisition:** a group set up by the Church for the prosecution of heretics
- **Moat:** a deep ditch around a castle or town, usually filled with water
- **Piety:** dutifulness in religion
- **Prophecy:** the foretelling or prediction of future events
- **Saint:** one known for piety or virtue

SIR WALTER RALEIGH

RHYMING RALEIGH

Born: c. 1554
South Devon, England
Died: October 29, 1618
London, England
64 years old

This is a little story about Sir Walter Raleigh. He was a small fry in the big sweep of history, but since he hung out with a woman who made unforgettable history, Queen Elizabeth I of England, his little story gets retold and retold. Raleigh was a shipbuilder, explorer, poet, soldier, Vice-Admiral of the Sea, and Captain of the Guard. To be these things, Raleigh had to pretend that he was in love with Queen Elizabeth. He had no problem bluffing about that and hedging the truth to get what he wanted, but when Elizabeth found out that he actually loved someone else and that he was secretly married, Elizabeth threw Sir Walter Raleigh in the slammer. He eventually got beheaded for a different matter, but that's another little story.

Young Walter grew up to be good at everything and afraid of

nothing. He went to college and was especially gifted at public speaking. He was confident and bold and could have been voted most likely to succeed, but as a man of the middle class, he had limited options, because leapfrogging into the upper classes wasn't allowed.

Walter became a soldier and a sailor, and he earned a reputation as a fearless man of action, but Raleigh wanted more. And just like in a fairy tale, Raleigh got his big break when he gallantly threw his coat over a puddle so Queen Elizabeth I wouldn't step in mud. Once Elizabeth had her foot on his coat, Raleigh had his foot in the door at the court of Elizabeth I.

Raleigh was just her type—tall, dark, and handsome. Elizabeth's court was a palace full of cute guys, because her advisors had been holding an endless Mr. Universe pageant of men from around the world for Elizabeth to choose from. They wanted her to get married and have an heir to the throne. Elizabeth had become an excellent judge of beefcake, but she wasn't going to get married. She had boyfriends to flirt and dance with, but she had no intention of saying "I do" to any of them, because a husband might chop her head off, just like her dad, Henry VIII, did to her mom and her stepmom. Elizabeth had a country to run, and she was married to the job. Dashing bachelors were just a hobby for her.

For the men it meant a lot more, and the idea that a nobody/wannabe like Raleigh was on royal turf annoyed the real nobility. They tried beating the crud out of Raleigh so he'd go away. Elizabeth loved having the men fight over her, so Raleigh stuck with it and earned his place in the competitive shark pool of good-looking suck-ups trying to win the position of Fantasy Beau to the queen. And it was worth it because if you got on Elizabeth's good side, she'd give you government jobs, titles, and other free stuff.

To chisel out a promising career, Raleigh had to follow the Rules for a Royal Suitor: laugh at all of Elizabeth's jokes, pretend to be in love with her, and don't marry anyone else, especially behind her back.

The twentysomething Raleigh and the fortysomething queen became an item. Raleigh didn't do the usual jousting and dancing like every other guy; instead, he liked literature, the French language, and dressing up. Elizabeth loved pearls, so Raleigh encrusted pearls on his shoes, put them in his hair, and bedazzled his doublets. He retooled his chatting skills and became a sweet-talking ladies' man able to woo his way up and over noblemen who outranked him. Raleigh's lovey-dovey poems addressed to Elizabeth made him irresistible.

Those eyes which set my fancy on a fire,

Those crisped hairs which hold my heart in chains,

Those dainty hands which conquered my desire,

That wit which of my thought does hold the reins!

With lines like these, Raleigh became Elizabeth's new Romeo. Elizabeth took this stuff seriously. She tossed aside last year's favorite dudes like they were old shoes so she could hang with the rhyming Raleigh.

Elizabeth started giving Raleigh moneymaking businesses, which made Raleigh extra poetic. He was put in charge of a company of footmen in Ireland, and he built ships for her, and in return she gave him estates and castles and constant face time. The more Elizabeth liked him, the less everyone else did. In a few short years, Raleigh was strutting around like he owned the place, and to get it all, he lied to Elizabeth's face as he waxed in verse.

See those sweet eyes, those more than sweetest eyes,

Eyes whom the stars exceed not in their grace.

He was no Shakespeare, but he was as good as any actor in one of Shakespeare's plays. Elizabeth was oblivious, and she let Raleigh found the first colony in the New World. He named it Virginia after the Virgin Queen: meaning Elizabeth. The other courtiers hoped

Raleigh would get lost at sea on the way to Virginia so they could swoop in, but Raleigh didn't even have to leave the safety of the Court to own it. Virginia was his.

Elizabeth's giving Raleigh a big piece of the New World enraged his rivals, and they called him "the best hated man in the world," because he was actually good at everything he did. He was even an excellent liar, because he was two-timing Elizabeth with girlfriends on the side. Elizabeth was living a romance and Raleigh was living the dream. He became the richest and most successful courtier in the land, and to top things off, Elizabeth knighted him. Now the competition had to call him *Sir* Walter Raleigh.

And just when they thought there wasn't anything else to give him, Sir Raleigh was appointed Captain of the Guard, aka head of Elizabeth's secret service. Now Raleigh was allowed into her private rooms, where she ate, slept, and hung out with her handpicked maids of honor/BFFs.

Raleigh kept the charade going for as long as he could.

> *My thoughts are winged with hopes, my hopes with love,*
> *Mount love unto the Moon in clearest night.*

Raleigh's golden pen continued to flow, but now the only thing he was actually mooning over was one of Elizabeth's maids of honor. Raleigh married his secret girlfriend, Elizabeth "Bess" Throckmorton, right under Elizabeth's nose.

The other courtiers finally devised a way to keep Raleigh from walking off with the entire kingdom and the New World too. Elizabeth was overdue for her next cute diversion. Their plan: bring on the young and handsome Earl of Essex.

Elizabeth was finally distracted with a new Romeo. Raleigh was getting elbowed out, and Essex was in.

Even though he was married, Raleigh's poor-me-I-still-love-you poems started rolling in.

> *If all the world and love were young*
> *And truth in every shepherd's tongue,*
> *These pretty pleasures might me move*
> *To live with thee and be thy love. . . .*

A poem he maybe should have penned:

On the sly I've secretly wed a maid of honor,
And I won't confess because I'd be a goner.

Meanwhile, the nineteen-year-old Earl of Essex was having trouble faking his side of the "I love you, you love me" game he was playing with the now fifty-four-year-old Elizabeth, so Elizabeth dumped him and took Raleigh back. This would have been a good time for Raleigh to figure out what rhymes with "wife," "baby on the way," "liar," "jerk," and "treason," which Raleigh and Bess had committed because they had wed without Elizabeth's consent.

Gossip went around London like there was Twitter, but no one wanted to tell Elizabeth she had been duped. Besides, it wasn't necessary because her maid of honor's stomach was going to be speaking for itself very soon.

But Bess was only allowed two weeks off without special permission, so she stayed as long as she could, and when she couldn't hide her pregnancy under the ruffles and geegaws any longer, Bess left court without a word and gave birth at her brother's house. Raleigh tried to skip town too, but Elizabeth ordered him to return.

Bess left the baby at her brother's house and returned to court like nothing was wrong. But pretty soon, Elizabeth's spies wanted to know who the two-month-old mystery baby was at Bess's brother's house, and Bess's brother was arrested.

Bess took the baby to Raleigh's house. They were a regular family—for a day.

Twenty-four hours later, Bess was taken away, and Raleigh was placed under house arrest, giving the rhymester time to write.

Like truthless dreams, so are my joys expired.

When he was interrogated, Raleigh denied he had a wife and said he loved the queen and no one else. The interrogator knew he was lying.

When Elizabeth finally realized Raleigh had played her for a fool, she retaliated with some poetic justice of her own. As any jilted lover might do if they could, Elizabeth threw Sir Walter Raleigh and Bess Throckmorton into the prison known as the Tower of London.

Elizabeth released Sir Walter Raleigh from prison after only a month so he could handle some official business for her. But it took about five years for Raleigh to regain access to the court, though he never won back Elizabeth's favor. Bess Throckmorton, Raleigh's wife, stayed in jail for four months and was banished from court forever. She and Raleigh moved to Sherborne Castle in Dorset.

Raleigh continued to write Elizabeth love notes; he didn't mention his wife in the notes for three years. Even after being caught, Sir Walter Raleigh stayed a chronic liar about love, fooling no one.

Turns out, there's only one real Rule for a Gentleman: don't be a liar.

SIR WALTER RALEIGH FACTS AND STATS

5 **OF ELIZABETH'S FAVORITE MEN:**

Raleigh wasn't the only one who married behind Elizabeth's back.

NAME	MARTIAL STATUS	EXECUTED
Robert Dudley, Earl of Leicester	secretly married	
Sir Christopher Hatton	never married	
Sir Walter Raleigh	secretly married	X
Sir Robert Cecil, Lord Burghley	approved marriage	
Robert Devereux, Earl of Essex	secretly married	X

500 **LINES** of verse written by Raleigh for Elizabeth while he was imprisoned in the Tower of London were never delivered to her.

359 **YEARS AFTER THE FACT,** the actual date of Raleigh's secret marriage was finally uncovered. In 1950, a diary belonging to Arthur Throckmorton (Bess's brother) was discovered in an outhouse. Sir Walter Raleigh and Bess Throckmorton were wed on November 19, 1591.

45 **MINUTES** was the duration of Sir Walter Raleigh's speech at his beheading. Raleigh was known for his speechifying.

15 YEARS was the length of time between Raleigh's sentencing for treason and his actual beheading. After Queen Elizabeth was dead, Raleigh was accused of plotting to dethrone King James I, and he was sent back to the Tower in 1603. His wife and ten-year-old second son came to live with him there. (His first son had died years earlier.) A third son was born while he was imprisoned. Sir Walter Raleigh was eventually beheaded on October 29, 1618.

 Raleigh's severed head was given to his wife, Bess Throckmorton.

TUDOR TUTORIAL

- **Elizabethan Era:** also known as the "Golden Age," an era marked by the reign of Elizabeth I of England (1558–1603)
- **Lady-in-Waiting:** married woman who attends to specific needs of a queen or a princess
- **Maid-of-Honor:** unmarried woman or young girl who does simple tasks for a queen or princess
- **Privy Chamber:** a private apartment in a royal residence
- **Tower of London:** a state prison in England for people accused of treason
- **Treason:** betraying the trust of a sovereign or state

CARAVAGGIO

THE BRUSH IS MIGHTIER THAN THE SWORD

Full name: Michelangelo
Merisi da Caravaggio
Born: September 1571
Caravaggio, Italy
Died: July 1610
Port'Ercole, Italy
39 years old

Artists are people too, and sometimes they mess up. It's not often that you hear about a great artist who was also a murderer, because if you were to go to a museum, no one would mention it. But here's the shading on the artist. Caravaggio could wield a sword as well as a paint-loaded brush. He split his time between painting master-pieces, brawling, kicking in doors, assaulting people, and serving jail time. He was wanted by the police for illegal weapons possession, and he was wanted by the pope to paint something for St. Peter's Cathedral in Rome. His violent life is mostly forgotten because his brush was mightier than his sword.

In 1571, Caravaggio was born into a middle-class family in the small town of Caravaggio, which is how he got his name. He was no art prodigy, but starting at thirteen, he moved away from home to be an artist's apprentice in Milan. For four years, his artistic talent blossomed along with his volatile personality. Besides learning to draw perspective, Caravaggio learned to draw blood. In the blink of an eye he could go from zero to vicious. There are rumors that he might have stabbed someone to death, but that's all we know about his adolescent years.

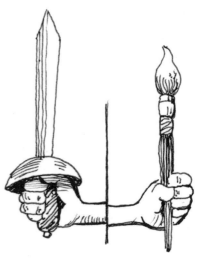

By the age of twenty-one, both his parents were dead. He quickly spent all his inheritance money and moved to Rome—art central—to live the life of a starving artist.

In spite of the aftereffects of plagues, famines, and a recent thorough sacking, Rome was back in business, especially the Catholic Church. The pope was on an art-shopping spree. The important assignments had been awarded to artists like the famous Michelangelo. Many of the other paintings were cranked out by artists in art factories—paintings of saints, resurrections, and crucifixions. Once you've seen one, you've seen them all, because artists were imprisoned for taking any artistic license. There was even a rulebook about how to paint for the pope. However, Caravaggio was not about following rules, and while he was on "fruit-painting detail" in one of these art factories, he painted moldy, wormy, rotten fruit—making it too real. This was noticed by the well-connected and art-loving Cardinal del Monte, who got Caravaggio out of the factory because it was a waste of his talent.

Even though del Monte noticed that Caravaggio was always on the verge of blowing his top, he introduced him to the people hiring artists to paint in churches, which was the only way an artist could get ahead. They liked Caravaggio's work, but his swordsmanship was improving neck and neck with his artistry. People tried to ignore the fact that he would paint for only two weeks, then spend two months getting into street fights, ending up in the hospital or in jail.

Everyone saw that he was gifted, and he'd be the first one to tell you if you didn't see it. But often his altarpieces were rejected because he didn't follow the art rules. He painted old Bible stories like they were current events. He was more interested in painting every Tom, Dick, and Harry with dirty feet than Jesus, Mary, and Joseph with halos. He showed the Virgin Mary on a bad hair day. He painted beggars, dead people, decapitated heads on platters, and lots of naked people. Artists had been painting naked people for centuries, but Caravaggio's skill with light, shadow, and skin tones made it look like real people were in the room. The Church didn't want people to see that. The more his paintings got rejected, the more famous he became, because there's nothing like telling people they can't look at something to make them really want to see it.

Being a famous artist back then was like being a rock star, and he acted like one. If anyone criticized his work, he went ballistic. Caravaggio was obsessed with status, and how to get more of it. But in the eyes of the nobility he was just a hired hand, a nobody. The most respected people were knights—and the most respected knights were the Knights of Malta. Caravaggio dreamed of being one. These knights had rulebooks too, and they believed the mark of true distinction was to "offend fearlessly," as in belittle, beat  up, ridicule, repeat—something Caravaggio longed to do. Generally knights were honorable but violent men.

Instead, Caravaggio got arrested for throwing stones, berating the police, battling on tennis courts, using obscene language, and carrying a weapon without a permit. And when his landlord kicked him out for not paying rent for four months, Caravaggio and a few of his friends pelted her house with stones.

Caravaggio got his big chance to get his artwork in St. Peter's alongside the likes of *the* Michelangelo. But Caravaggio painted bare feet and someone missing their clothes again. The painting was removed after one month.

He had a knack for being a screwup. During a tennis match, Caravaggio got into a tussle with the other player. It started with hitting

each other with tennis rackets and ended with Caravaggio stabbing the other man to death with a sword. And he wasn't going to get away with it. The pope had just taken down Caravaggio's painting; now he was going to take down the man with a *banda capitale,* a decree that meant anyone, anywhere, could kill Caravaggio on sight. With the pope's blessing, Caravaggio was a walking target.

Caravaggio fled to Naples. The art community was thrilled he came. Pope's orders or not, no one wanted to kill the genius painter they had heard so much about. They escorted him straight to an easel.

But Caravaggio knew he was living on borrowed time. To save his career and his life, he saw knighthood as a way to possibly redeem himself.

It was a long shot, but he figured he had nothing to lose, so he went to the island of Malta—sect headquarters. Knights were from the wealthiest families in Europe. They took vows of chastity, obedience, and other un-fun things. They dedicated themselves to the defense of the Catholic faith against the infidel . . . or a painter. To do this, they were allowed to beat the crud out of anybody they felt like. And as a rule, tennis court murderers were not welcome in the brotherhood.

Not easily discouraged, Caravaggio got to work painting a very flattering full-length portrait of the Grand Master of the Knights, attempting to paint his way into the group.

Many, many paintings later, Caravaggio was allowed to sign up for knight classes. He must have studied really hard because he became a Knight in Obedience. In return, his murder charge was erased. He got the Knight frock, and the freedom to act superior. The hefty initiation fee was paid off with a masterpiece: *The Beheading of St. John the Baptist.* But real Knights still thought of Caravaggio as a nobody—a faker.

Things went smoothly for four months until Caravaggio's obedience, Knight training, and self-control gave out and he picked a fight with another Knight—a no-no in the rulebook. He was dumped in an eleven-foot-deep hole, a place where troublemakers were left to die.

Always thinking out of the box, he escaped the hole, probably with the help of one of the few art-loving Knights. Then he sailed off the island, breaking another Knight rule—don't leave Malta without permission. The Knights voted unanimously to kick Caravaggio out of the "'hood." If Caravaggio hadn't disappeared, they would have defrocked him right in front of his latest beheading painting.

Caravaggio really had something to fear now, as the *banda capitale* was nothing compared to angry Knights who didn't care one little bit about his painting talent: guys who crusaded, and signed oaths, but couldn't date.

With the wild bunch on his tail, Caravaggio slept with his dagger at his side. Now he painted as if his life depended on it, because it did. He sent paintings back to Rome to buy himself a pardon, and he sent paintings to the Grand Master of the Knights so that he might call off the brotherhood. It didn't work.

He was working his way back to Rome when he was caught by four knight types who decided that his painting days were over. They tried to kill him, but they only killed his looks. His face was so badly beaten that afterward he was unrecognizable. The quasi knights tried to even the score, an eye for an eye, because no one should get away with murder, not even a talented artist.

But Caravaggio had a few more great paintings in him, including *David with the Head of Goliath.* In the painting, Caravaggio painted his own face (pre-knight attack) on the decapitated head of Goliath.

Not too long after, Caravaggio died of a fever. He was only thirty-nine years old. He never made it back to Rome.

Ultimately, Caravaggio's criminal behavior caught up to him, and justice for his crime was leveled in the streets. He had a genius imagination and artistic talent to match, but it didn't matter—he was a murderer. Too bad Caravaggio didn't know that his brush was much mightier than his sword.

CARAVAGGIO FACTS AND STATS

BAROQUE ART:

Baroque style (Italy, 1600 to late 1700s) is realistic, very ornate, and dramatic, with a sharp contrast of lights and darks. Objects are in motion and close to the viewer and focus on religious themes.

8 BAROQUE ARTISTS AND SCULPTORS:

- Gian Lorenzo Bernini (1598–1680)
- Caravaggio (1571–1610)
- Annibale Carracci (1560–1609)
- Francois Duquesnoy (1597–1643)
- Rembrandt (1606–1669)
- Peter Paul Rubens (1577–1640)
- Diego Velázquez (1599–1660)
- Jan Vermeer (1632–1675)

4 YEARS CARAVAGGIO SPENT in exile and on the run after he murdered a man on a tennis court. He kept his dagger by his side even in bed when he slept.

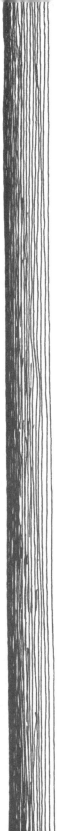

0 DRAWINGS of Caravaggio's have ever been found, only paintings.

0 LETTERS of Caravaggio's have survived.

9 PREREQUISITES for joining the Knights of Malta:

- Legitimacy of nobility, blood, and descent
- Not a member of another order
- Unmarried
- Virtuous life
- Not in debt
- At least sixteen years old
- Good physical and mental health
- Capable of bearing arms
- Wealthy

ACCEPTABLE KNIGHT BEHAVIOR:

Caravaggio lived in Rome when skill at swordsmanship was the key to honor and a symbol of social status and of a man's value.

"Attack him with your dagger, and plunge it into that ill-borne breast . . . thrust at him your knife, and color it in the biggest vein of his hot red blood . . . make him fall to the earth like a sack of straw."
—*A Knight's Duties* by Tommaso d'Alessandri

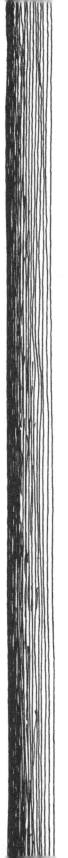

2010, **A PARTICULARLY IMPORTANT YEAR,** in that scientists announced that they had most likely (85 percent sure) found Caravaggio's remains. After studying his bones, it was determined that he probably died from a toxic level of lead, which perhaps came from his paints.

2014, **APPROXIMATELY FOUR HUNDRED YEARS** after he died, a Caravaggio painting may have been found in a locked, leaky attic in France. The beheading scene gave it away. Art experts are mixed about the painting's authenticity.

CARAVAGGIO'S PALETTE

- **Carbon Black:** made by burning bones and wood
- **Lead White:** Pieces of lead and vinegar were placed in a jug, and then the jug was buried in a pit and covered with dung to create heat, which formed a white substance on the lead—it was very toxic.
- **Madder Lake:** a red color made from the madder plant after it is dried, crushed, and boiled
- **Rabbit Skin Glue:** made by boiling rabbit tendons, cartilage, and skin; used for preparing canvas for painting
- **Yellow Ochre:** made from yellow dirt and is known as an earth color

BLACKBEARD

BURNING MAN

Real Name: Edward
Teach (Thatch)
Born: c. 1680
near Bristol, England
Died: November 22, 1718
North Carolina, United States
38 years old

As we know from movies and Halloween costumes, pirates wore cool clothes. The best-dressed pirate was Blackbeard. He didn't need a patch, a hook, or a peg leg to scare everybody to death; he used pyrotechnics. But it was just a flashy show of fire and smoke. Blackbeard captured over a hundred ships and he never killed a single prisoner. Except for the stealing, kidnapping, and destroying of property, he wasn't that bad.

Most pirates had the basic model, skull-and-crossbones flag, but Blackbeard's signature flag depicted a skeleton stabbing a bloody red heart while drinking at the same time. It went better with his outfit. It also made him stand out from the crowd, which worked great—until it didn't.

Back in 1702, practically every country in Europe was ferrying boatloads of gold, sugar, ivory, and gems across the ocean from the New World. It was only a matter of time before the royalty of England, Spain, and France wanted to steal each other's stuff. The capturing and pillaging of treasure-loaded ships was a legal profession called privateering.

Before Blackbeard was Blackbeard he was just Ed. And Ed was a sailor on board an English privateering ship. Sailors were treated no better than captive criminals, and they lived in fear of mouth rot, drowning, and death by weather. Forty percent died en route. Every weensy meal had a good chance of being their last supper. They were barely paid, and captains were cruel and flogged their men for the slightest mistake. Home sweet home was belowdecks, shoehorned in a hammock, swinging over rotting provi-

sions. After twelve years of risking his life at sea, and with nothing to show for it, Ed made a career adjustment.

He kept doing what his country had trained him to do, but with some splashy re-branding. Since hair practically sprouted out of his eyeballs and "like a frightful meteor, covered his whole face," he changed his name to Blackbeard. He designed a flag and switched his job title from privateer to pirate. Yo-ho-why not? Now he kept what he stole instead of giving it to England, and he got to work learning how to braid his beard.

On the downside of going pirate, Blackbeard would be arrested if he went back to England or to any country with a government. On the upside, the islands in the Caribbean were government-free, so he was able to dock at places that are now resort locations. And yo-ho-ho, it was said he had a wife in almost every port, or at least in fourteen of them. And best of all, pirates shared the wealth; whatever was stolen was evenly split among the crew. Captains were chosen by popular vote, so pirates were treated well.

Eventually, Blackbeard was aye-ayed in as captain of five ships and seven hundred men. If a ship approached his, Blackbeard dressed for the occasion. He based his outfit around the three pistols holstered in a sash across his chest. His braided hair and beard were tied with ribbons. He tucked long fuses under his hat and lit them so his head was engulfed in a fiery glow and a plume of smoke. His backup pirates worked up to something quite spectacular too, running around like wild animals, so that by the time the target ship came near, its crew took one look, dropped sail, and surrendered. He perfected the psychological warfare of fear with the Blackbeard Show because the last thing he wanted to do was drown a bunch of sailors just like him. He had

other plans. After taking what he wanted and burning the looted ship, he'd give a motivational talk to the captured sailors about the joys of piracy—as in lots of rum and fun. Those who didn't sign up were dropped off on the nearest shore, which was okay because they'd eventually go home and talk about him.

In 1717, word of mouth about Blackbeard's smoking head and the amount of booty he was stealing from King George I of England was enough to convince the king to forgive pirates of all their crimes, as long as they retired. Pirates could keep all their stolen treasure too. Blackbeard got a second chance to start a legit life as a rich man.

But what could Blackbeard possibly do on land where he could still light his beard on fire? Who would he intimidate? What would he wear? The Blackbeard Show didn't close, but hundreds of his men left to secure their pardons. The Blackbeard production was trimmed to one ship and one hundred men. He relocated and found a new investor—the governor of North Carolina. But now he was a hunted man with a bounty on his distinctive and very recognizable head.

The governor of Virginia knew Blackbeard was docked in North Carolina, and he was sick of Blackbeard seizing so many ships along the American colonies. Even though it was completely illegal to attack another colony, Virginia's governor sent two sloops (small sailboats) packed to the gills with 120 men to kill Blackbeard.

Blackbeard was warned they were coming, but he was too busy hosting a pirate party on his ship. He was also too drunk to notice when the two sloops anchored nearby. His party went on all night long. Yo-ho-YOLO.

In charge of one of the sloops was Lieutenant Robert Maynard. In the morning, Maynard sent some men in a rowboat to get intel before they made their attack.

The party was still going and a few blotto pirates shot wildly at the rowboat, which officially ruined Maynard's surprise attack.

Now, as a bunch of pirates watched, Maynard's two sloops lifted anchor. The timing was all wrong. There was no wind, so no sailing; the sloops didn't go anywhere. The crew manned the oars and started paddling, but they paddled the ships right into the mud and got stuck. Waiting for high tide or a tow wasn't an option, so they started throwing things overboard until the ships eventually floated free.

All the splashing got Blackbeard's impaired attention. With a drink in his hand, and just like a pirate, he hollered a bad word, then demanded, "Villains, who are you and from whence came you?" From what he was seeing of their seamanship, Blackbeard wasn't too concerned. Besides, he had eight cannons; the little sloops didn't have any.

As they paddled closer to Blackbeard, he finally noticed the curiously large number of sailors crowded on board the sloops. He sobered up the best he could, and his crew loaded the guns with lead shot, nails, chunks of old iron, and other stuff that hurts when it hits, and then they blasted away.

When the smoke cleared, Blackbeard saw one sloop damaged beyond repair. The other sloop was intact. Some wounded men were down; only two men were still standing. But Blackbeard failed to put two and two together, making a case for "Don't drink and do math." Where did he think everybody had gone?

Blackbeard and ten of his pirates hopped on board the sloop with the two men to see what they could steal.

The surprise attack wasn't totally ruined. As soon as Blackbeard's feet hit the deck, a dozen or more of Maynard's men jumped out of hiding and attacked him.

Maynard took the first stab at Blackbeard, but his sword slammed right into Blackbeard's ammo box, hurting only his sword. Blackbeard took a swipe at Maynard with his sword. Then Maynard shot Blackbeard with his gun. Who knows why Maynard didn't do that first, but anyway, the shot didn't kill Blackbeard. Another man slashed Blackbeard's face with a sword.

Blackbeard kept fighting even after being shot five times and stabbed twenty times. His flair for the dramatic was still with him, but he lost the fight when he lost his head.

The whole hand-to-hand fight took less than six minutes.

All ten men in Blackbeard's boarding party were killed.

Blackbeard's detached head was hung from the prow at the front of his ship, near where the carved mermaid sometimes goes. What was left of him was thrown into the ocean.

With Blackbeard's hairy head still attached, his ship was sailed around for a month and a half on a victory tour until Maynard gave the head to the Virginia governor. The governor then put Blackbeard's head on a stick on the shore of the Hampton River at a place still known today as Blackbeard's Point, although his head is long gone. There's a rumor that his skull was later used as a cup.

England had trained Blackbeard to be a pirate, but he did it his own way. Blackbeard was a trendsetter, and his iconic image has lasted centuries. All the other pirates were poseurs.

Once you've been Blackbeard, there's no blending in, even if you want to.

And yo, some pirates were bad, but not Blackbeard. Remember, he never killed anybody.

Who knew?

BLACKBEARD FACTS AND STATS

THE JOLLY ROGER PIRATE FLAG:
The best-known pirate flag is the skull and crossbones, known as the Jolly Roger. But it wasn't the only one. Pirate flags were usually black, red, and white. The black symbolized death, and red symbolized battle. The most common images on the flags were skulls, skeletons, swords, spears, and hourglasses. The intention was to strike fear in their enemies.

75 PERCENT OF THE EARTH IS WATER. And even though oceans are the major feature of our planet, they're easy to forget. We fly over them in airplanes or surf near the shore. But just like in Blackbeard's time, their main use for humans is for moving merchandise from place to place.

90 PERCENT OF EVERYTHING you eat, wear, strum, sit on, drink from, or play with has traveled to you in a cargo ship.

100,000 CARGO SHIPS are crossing the oceans every day. Pirates are out there too.

3 MILLION SHIPS are at the bottom of the world's oceans. Most of those ships will never be found. Blackbeard's most famous ship was *Queen Anne's Revenge.* It ran aground in June 1718, a few months before he was killed.

1996 WAS THE YEAR the *Queen Anne's Revenge* was discovered near Beaufort Inlet, North Carolina.

12 RECOVERED ITEMS:

- Anchors
- Brass buttons
- Cannonballs
- Cannons
- Coins with the image of Queen Anne
- Fishing weights
- Glass beads
- Grenades
- Navigation tools
- Pewter spoons
- Shackles
- Wineglasses

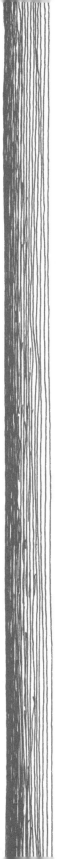

100 POUNDS reward was offered for catching Blackbeard. That's worth about $25,000 today.

> *. . . For Edward Teach, commonly called Captain Teach, or Blackbeard, one hundred Pounds, for every other Commander of a Pyrate Ship, Sloop, or Vessel, forty pounds; for every Lieutenant, Master, or Quarter-Master Boatswain, or Carpenter, twenty Pounds; for every other inferior Officer, fifteen Pounds, and for every private Man taken on Board such Ship, Sloop, or Vessel, ten Pounds.*

 18 months was about the length of Blackbeard's pirate career.

PIRATES' AND MARINERS' LINGO

- **Adrift:** floating free
- **Aft:** the back of a ship
- **Blaggard:** a man you can't trust
- **Bounty:** a reward
- **Cackle Fruit:** chicken eggs
- **Deadlights:** eyes
- **Fore:** the front of a ship
- **Grog:** rum mixed with water
- **Grub:** food
- **Haven:** a safe place
- **Hornswoggle:** to cheat

JOHN WILKES BOOTH

LEADING BAD GUY

Born: May 10, 1838
near Bel Air, Maryland
Died: April 26, 1865
Port Royal, Virginia
26 years old

Most criminals run away from the scene of a crime, but John Wilkes Booth made a big entrance in a scene that wasn't even in the script. He thought he'd be a hero for killing President Abraham Lincoln. As you may have heard, he did it in a crowded theater, and then he jumped from the presidential box eleven feet down onto the stage as if he expected applause for having shot Lincoln in the back of the head. The only standing ovation he got was the people yelling, "Stop that man!"

As a boy John was known for shooting and torturing cats. If a kid did that today, it would be a tip-off to tell a grown-up. Not that Booth was the kind to sit and listen, and the grown-ups at home weren't much better. Booth's alcoholic father shot a man in the face, tried to sell John's brother Edwin for five dollars, and had a "secret" family on the side—and the one John grew up in wasn't the legal one. John's report cards were okay, and he was popular, but he was wild. Tattoos were rare in the mid-1800s, but at thirteen, Booth tattooed himself on his left hand with India ink, writing JWB, surrounded by a halo of stars.

His drunk father was a famous actor and so were two of John's brothers. Sharing the stage wasn't for John; he came up with a killer one-man show, making sure he'd be the only Booth anyone remembered, like the non-erasable tattooed stars on his hand. Professional acting was just a pit stop for Booth; hating Lincoln was his real job.

When the Civil War ended, so did Booth's original plot to kidnap President Lincoln. Booth had been planning to exchange Lincoln for Confederate POWs with a small group of Southern sympathizers he had recruited for the job. But when Booth-the-cat-killer heard that Lincoln was going to give black Americans the right to vote, Booth made a new plan.

On April 14, 1865, Booth wrote a three-page manifesto, rented a getaway horse, and planned his big entrance to turn the comedy *Our American Cousin*—playing at Ford's Theatre in Washington, D.C.—into *Our American Tragedy*.

Neither President Lincoln nor Booth was at the theater when the play started. Booth was binge drinking at the bar next door. Eleven minutes into act 1, when Lincoln arrived with his wife, Mary, and their guests Clara Harris and Major Henry Rathbone, the play stopped and the orchestra broke into "Hail to the Chief." Booth arrived humming to himself for the final act of the play.

Since there was no such thing as the Secret Service yet, Booth had no problem getting into the presidential box. When he heard the actor's line "Well, I guess I know enough to turn you inside out, old gal," John Wilkes Booth cried, "Freedom!" and shot President Abraham Lincoln behind the left ear with his one-bullet gun. Lincoln died the next morning.

Normal murderers run away; Booth stuck around for a "Ta-da!" moment. He hollered, *"Sic semper tyrannis!"* ("Ever thus to tyrants!") as he jumped onto the stage. Major Rathbone had almost stopped Booth before he jumped from the railing, knocking Booth off course enough for his spurs to snag the American flag hanging there as he dropped down.

Booth made his eye-popping stage entrance on all fours. He broke his left fibula in half, two inches above his ankle, which should have made catching him easy, except no one was sure what had just happened. No one had ever

shot a U.S. president before. "The South is avenged. I—I—I have done it!" Booth said, and hop-stepped to the wings and out the alley door.

Without thinking, Booth shoved away the teenager holding his rented horse, but because of his injury, he struggled to get on the horse and almost got caught again, this time by an audience member who had sprinted out the back door to stop him.

Booth's parting words, *Sic semper tyrannis,* were a good clue. That was Virginia's state motto, and it was exactly where Booth was going. But nobody got it.

Getting to Virginia required crossing the closed Navy Yard Bridge into Maryland, but the guards didn't know anything about the assassination yet, so they let Booth through. Then Booth met up with David Herold, one of his co-conspirators who was his guide to Virginia. He had gotten across the bridge too.

Still luckier, Booth passed two military forts before they received a telegraph with the news.

But Booth was so proud, he started spreading the news himself. "We have assassinated the president," he told the unsuspecting landlord at the Surratt Tavern when he picked up the two guns the Surratts, co-conspirators and owners of the tavern, had let him stash earlier.

Back in Washington, D.C., the War Department called in the military, the police, and the best detectives in the country. Boats and roads out of Washington were blocked; too bad Booth had already left town. Booth's theater buddies took the heat. The actors and stagehands at Ford's Theatre were forced to do a reenactment of *Our American Cousin* for an audience of investigators so they could look for clues. One stagehand was arrested, and so were other friends of Booth's.

Everything was going like clockwork for Booth, except for his broken leg. Skedaddling to Virginia was scrapped for a five-hour detour to see Dr. Samuel Mudd in Maryland. Mudd set Booth's broken leg, chiseled out a crutch for him, and gave Booth a shaving kit so he could change his looks, because the morning newspapers described his downturned mustache. Booth also saw all the bad assassination reviews.

Bad reviews didn't fit Booth's heroic delusions. He was in shock, along with everybody else in America, but for opposite reasons. There would be no glory or applause, only a mangled leg and a manhunt closing in. Booth stayed on the move. He had been counting on his kidnapping co-conspirators to help him along the way, but most of them didn't want anything to do with Booth now that he had murdered the president. Booth was reduced to sleeping in the woods.

Booth and Herold crouched under bushes while the cavalry galloped by looking for them. They could hide quietly, but their neighing horses couldn't. The only way to keep the horses quiet was to shoot them. That's a bloody and cruel version of shooting out all the tires on the getaway car. Booth's broken-legged escape came to a screeching dead stop.

Finally a willing Southern sympathizer took Booth and Herold to a little boat with one paddle and a broken oar on the Potomac River so they could row to Virginia. It took two tries figuring out the right way to row across the river at night unseen by the gunboats full of soldiers and detectives.

More than a week after the assassination, Booth finally got to Virginia. He thought he was home free.

But Virginians didn't want anything to do with him either. Sick of sleeping outside, getting nowhere, and being kicked out of people's homes, Booth forced a freeborn black farmer at knifepoint into putting him up for the night. The next day, Booth made the farmer take him in a horse-drawn cart to the ferryboat landing in Port Conway, Virginia.

Booth thought he was putting distance between him and the manhunt, which he thought was as far off as New York, Pennsylvania, and Missouri, but this was really the beginning of the end.

Booth and Herold were dropped near the home of William Rollins. Rollins saw Booth and Herold and then watched three teenaged former Confederate soldiers, including one he recognized named Private William S. Jett, ride up to them.

Believing these Southern boys would like what he did and not turn him in, Booth boasted about being Lincoln's assassin and that the reward for catching him was $175,000, which was a $75,000 exaggeration.

The three boys wanted to help. They were impressed by Booth's swollen, blackish leg with the bone coming out, prompting one of the boys to loan Booth his horse as they took Booth and Herold on a ferryboat ride across the Rappahannock River. It was against boat rules to stay mounted, but Booth didn't get off the horse, and he stood out like, well, a guy on a horse in a boat.

When they landed on the opposite bank, Herold went off to look for supplies, and Jett took Booth to Richard H. Garrett's farm.

Back in Washington, detectives received a telegraph with a tip that Booth was in Virginia, and the Sixteenth New York Cavalry of twenty-seven men and two detectives hit the road to apprehend him.

The only reason the Garretts let Booth stay was that he lied about being a Confederate soldier named Boyd. The Garretts felt sorry for this Boyd guy because he was wounded, in pain, and looked like he'd been living outside, so they allowed him to sleep in their home. But then Booth showed them his JWB tattoo, and at dinner told them he thought that Booth shot Lincoln "for notoriety's sake," revealing a lot about himself and disturbing the Garretts a ton.

The Garretts were already suspicious of Booth, but when Herold arrived the next day with a repeating rifle that could shoot seven shots in a row (a big deal back then), the Garretts told them to leave.

Horseless houseguests are a real burden, and the Garretts were going to have to transport Booth and Herold out of there to get rid of them. The Garretts tried to rent a wagon from a neighbor, but without luck. It was getting dark, so the Garretts escorted their guests into the barn for the night and secretly locked them inside.

Little did Booth know he had been spotted days earlier while sitting high on the horse on the Port Conway ferry. Rollins told the authorities that Private Jett had taken Booth on a ferryboat ride. When questioned, Jett caved, which made catching Booth a lot easier. He led the Sixteenth New York Cavalry to the Garretts' farm, right where he had dropped Booth off.

By two a.m., the locked barn was surrounded. Booth wouldn't surrender, so the detectives set the barn on fire.

Herold gave up, while Booth took on the pointless project of attempting to stomp out the fire with only one good foot. It didn't take long until the whole barn was ablaze.

Tired of waiting for Booth to step out with his hands up, Sergeant Boston Corbett aimed his gun through an opening in the wall and shot Booth right through the neck, immediately paralyzing him from the neck down.

The show was over.

Booth was dragged out of the inferno. It was a bit late to check their work, but to make extra sure it was Booth, the detectives matched Booth's face to a photograph, compared the details on the reward poster, and examined his tattoo.

They had gotten their man.

About three hours later, a doctor arrived and stuck a bullet probe in Booth's neck wound, which was a waste since the bullet had gone straight through Booth's body. The assassin died soon after.

Even at the end, Booth didn't acknowledge that he was the villain in an American tragedy and never said he was sorry. Booth was fighting for a dead cause. He killed a beloved president who had been leading America in a positive direction. Booth changed history, but not in the way he imagined. Booth's stage career is forgotten, but if you're looking for a leading villain in American history, Booth is your man.

JOHN WILKES BOOTH FACTS AND STATS

2 GUNS were found on Booth when he was caught—a Colt revolver and a Spencer carbine.

12 OTHER ITEMS found in Booth's possession:

- Calling cards of five women
- Catholic Agnus Dei medal
- Compass
- Diary
- Keys
- Matches
- Money
- Pipe
- Pocketknife
- Silver horseshoe charm
- Small onions
- Tobacco

$100,000 REWARD for Booth and two of his conspirators is worth $1,404,517 in today's money ($50,000 for Booth, $25,000 for David Herold, $25,000 for John Surratt).

$75,000 REWARD MONEY for Booth and Herold was paid in part to these men:

- Colonel Lafayette Baker: $3,750
- Detective Luther Byron Baker: $4,000
- Detective Everton Judson Conger: $4,000
- Sergeant Boston Corbett: $2,545
- First Lieutenant Edward P. Doherty: $7,500
- Sergeant Andrew Wendell: $2,545

The rest of the money went to the members of the Sixteenth New York Cavalry.

1,700 EYEWITNESSES were at Ford's Theatre when John Wilkes Booth killed President Abraham Lincoln.

2 FAILED ATTEMPTS by Booth's co-conspirators to assassinate other members of the government happened the same night Booth killed Lincoln. George Azterodt attempted to kill Vice President Andrew Johnson, and Lewis Powell tried to kill Secretary of State William Seward.

4 OF BOOTH'S CO-CONSPIRATORS were hanged:

- George Azterodt
- Lewis Powell
- David Herold
- Mary Surratt

4 PRESIDENTIAL ASSASSINATIONS have been committed in the United States of America:

- Abraham Lincoln, on April 14, 1865, by John Wilkes Booth
- James Garfield, on July 2, 1881, by Charles J. Guiteau
- William McKinley, on September 6, 1901, by Leon Czolgosz
- John F. Kennedy, on November 22, 1963, by Lee Harvey Oswald

BOOTH'S ESCAPE ROUTE

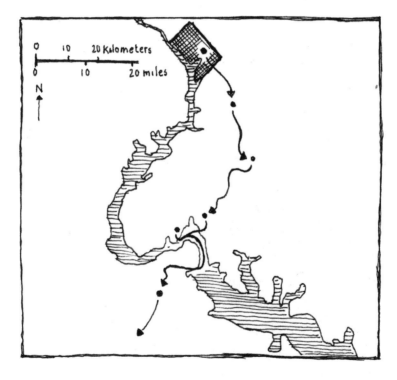

JESSE JAMES

MOMMA'S BOY

Born: September 27, 1847
Clay County, Missouri
Died: April 3, 1882
St. Joseph, Missouri
34 years old

You just can't get a better name for a criminal than Jesse James. It doesn't mean he was a cool outlaw; he wasn't exactly Robin Hood, but he had a knack for self-promotion—1800s style. Today, he'd have millions of Snapchat and Twitter followers watching his train wreck of a life. Back then, he'd rob a train and hand the one engineer that he *hadn't* shot a press release explaining his reasons for doing it. It made him famous, and he liked it, but maybe he would have lived longer if he hadn't been famous.

Jesse was a momma's boy. His six-foot-tall, large-and-in-charge mom liked to give orders, and Jesse obeyed. Her practical jokes weren't for laughs but "a way to get even." Everything was either her way or the dirt highway out of there. Jesse's dad took the highway, but he died a few months later. Jesse's mom remarried a doctor, but the first thing she had him do was quit medicine so he could help oversee her farm and the seven slaves she owned.

Back then, slavery was legal in Missouri, but not everybody agreed with it. During the Civil War, Missouri was a Border State—one of only four slave states that did not separate from the Union—and it had characteristics of both the North and the South. Everybody in Missouri had a different opinion about the right to own slaves. You kept your friends close and your enemy neighbors in your gun sights.

At sixteen, Jesse joined his older brother, Frank, in an illegal gang of guerrilla fighters to further the Southern cause and to protect his mom's way of life. The guerrillas were a bunch of local guys resisting Northern occupation by going on killing sprees. Their surprise attacks and frequent hiding in bushes earned them the nickname "bushwhackers." His mom sent Jesse off in a newly sewn guerrilla shirt for him to wear while he wreaked havoc with guys like "Bloody

Bill" Anderson, known for scalping his victims. These proslavery boys firebombed houses, held neighbors prisoner, and killed people. Jesse's mom hid the boy thugs, and the sheriff had to warn people about going to the Jameses' farm: "The old woman would kill you if the boys don't."

The Civil War ended and Jesse's side lost, but he wasn't ready to give up. At nineteen, outshining his older brother, Frank, Jesse became the leader of a gang of Southern ex-guerrillas to keep up the fight. The gang robbed Northern-owned banks in broad daylight instead of at night like other thieves, and they derailed trains out in the middle of nowhere. Or they'd stop a stagecoach and take all the passengers' jewelry and money. Jesse might pistol-whip or shoot a person, it just depended on his mood.

Sometimes Jesse James robbed trains while wearing a Ku Klux Klan mask, and Southern newspapers printed his letters spewing hatred and boasting about his gang. Fellow gang members wanted Jesse to lie low and stop using their names in print; he was getting them killed. Jesse's psycho-mom-gone-guerrilla was using his gang members' names too—she'd name her newborns after the dead ones.

Finally, Jesse James's robberies, murders, and ongoing press campaign made him a recognized and wanted man. The reward for his capture was five hundred dollars—two hundred more than the regular going rate for nabbing a bad guy.

Sheriffs assembled posses of armed citizens, and Pinkerton's National Detective Agency hunted for his gang, now known as the James-Younger Gang because Jesse and his brother had joined forces with four brothers from the Younger family. But Jesse's knowledge of every back road and secret hiding nook in Missouri made him uncatchable. Plus he had his mom, Zerelda. Family meant so much to him that he married his first cousin, the one who was named after his mom. (They might have been the last two Zereldas ever.) Mother-in-law issues aside, bride Zerelda must have suspected she'd outlive Jesse by a long shot thanks to his line of work.

Jesse became even more reckless and unpredictable, and the gang got noticeably smaller as members quit, got caught, or died on the job. And finding people willing to hide Jesse and the guys was getting harder and harder. It was time for Jesse to take early retirement.

Except being famous made retiring difficult, something Jesse should have thought of earlier. He moved his growing family out of Missouri, changed his name to John Davis Howard, and pretended to be a regular guy. But just in case, he kept two horses saddled up at all times, and he never took off his guns, even inside his house. Jesse was a failure at being a nobody, and he was bored to death.

After three years of blowing a bunch of money gambling, Jesse went back into the family thieving business.

He wrangled up a new gang and robbed a train. He had missed the spotlight so much that he handed the train's telegraph operator a press release that he had written for the *Kansas City Journal*. "We are the boys that are hard to handle and will make it hot for the party that ever tries

to take us." And he named everyone in his gang, just like he used to. Except by this time, Jesse was old news, and the Civil War was long over.

Being less loved by the public made Jesse pouty, and he compulsively went from crime to crime. His brother always came with him, but the new gang wasn't the same; they fought with each other, and Jesse didn't trust them. For safety, Jesse disguised himself by dyeing his beard black, and he moved his family after every heist, from Kentucky to Tennessee and back to Missouri again. Even when the local sheriff knew Jesse was nearby, he wouldn't arrest the outlaw to avoid being gunned down by one of the violent Jesse James supporters who might still be lurking nearby.

Then Jesse killed another person in Missouri during a train robbery. He had to be stopped. Six railroad companies, the United States

Express Company, a gunpowder firm, and the governor pooled their money. The reward for catching Jesse James was now $10,000—a fortune worth about a quarter of a million dollars today.

This was fine with Jesse because to him there was no such thing as bad press. He derailed another train, robbed everybody, and then took a bow, like he expected everybody to clap. Once again, he was in the spotlight and the star of his little gang. But it wasn't the same. His latest gang members didn't share the same allegiance to the Confederate cause as Jesse had with his ex-guerrilla buddies. They surrendered to authorities and agreed to testify against Jesse. But first he had to be caught.

His brother Frank stuck with him—brothers could be trusted (and outshined). His newest gang members were also brothers, Charlie and Bob Ford. They moved in with Jesse while he planned the next holdup.

It turns out the kind of brotherly love the Ford boys were feeling was inspired by the $10,000 reward money—half paid on capture, half on conviction. On the sly, Bob Ford made a deal with Missouri

Governor Thomas T. Crittenden: in exchange for Jesse James, Bob wouldn't get punished for his crimes and he'd get the reward money.

The Fords got their chance on April 3, 1882. Feeling hot, Jesse took off his coat and vest, which revealed his guns underneath. Jesse was going in and out of the house and he worried a neighbor would see his guns, so he took them off too, which was a first. Jesse decided, for possibly the first time also, to do a little housekeeping. He took a brush and pushed a chair up to the wall that had a picture hanging on it. Jesse stepped up on the chair and began to dust the picture. Bob and Charlie took one look at each other and pulled out their guns. Bob shot Jesse James in the back of the head.

Jesse James was dead at thirty-four years old.

Many people refused to believe that he was really dead.

Two thousand people came to glimpse the outlaw's dead body before it was put in the ground at his mom's house. Gold watches, stickpins, horses, and other stuff that Jesse had pinched were returned to their rightful owners.

Since the Fords killed Jesse instead of capturing him, they were convicted of murder. Governor Crittenden pardoned them, and they received some reward money. But the public wouldn't let the Fords forget the cowardly way they had killed Jesse James. Charlie Ford eventually killed himself. Bob Ford starred in a vaudeville show, *How I Shot Jesse James,* for a short time until eventually someone shot him dead too.

Frank James turned himself in and was acquitted of all his crimes. Jesse's wife died in 1900. As for Jesse's mom, not long after Jesse's demise, she said, "They have killed him on whom I depended, and I have got to have money." Turns out she continued to depend on him; she spent the next few decades charging people a fee to see Jesse James's grave and retelling his story.

JESSE JAMES FACTS AND STATS

10 MEMBERS of the James-Younger Gang:

Jesse James	John Younger
Frank James	Clell Miller
Bob Younger	Arthur McCoy
Cole Younger	Charlie Pitts
Jim Younger	Bill Chadwell

5 FACTS about posses:

1. The term "posse" comes from *posse comitatus,* meaning the power of the county.

2. The sheriff has the authority to call the power of the county/body of men to enforce the law.

3. Posse duty used to be mandatory and considered a right of responsible citizens if you were called to it, like serving on a jury today.

4. There was no pay for posse work unless there was a reward and the sheriff decided to share it.

5. Sheriffs' posses still exist today, although today's posse members are volunteers.

1ST NATIONAL DETECTIVE AGENCY in the United States

was called Pinkerton's National Detective Agency (1850). They were hired to catch Jesse James.

1ST FEMALE DETECTIVE in the United States was Kate Warne. She was hired in 1856 by the Pinkerton Agency.

1ST AFRICAN AMERICAN DETECTIVE in the United States was John Scobell. He was hired in 1862 by the Pinkerton Agency.

The Pinkerton logo with the eye and the words "We never sleep" inspired the nickname for a detective, "private eye."

3 PINKERTON DETECTIVES were killed by Jesse James and his gang.

2 TEETH AND 2 HAIRS from Jesse's original gravesite helped to prove that the real Jesse James was buried there. Many Jesse James imposters turned up over the years, but in 1996, DNA tests confirmed that he was indeed dead. His DNA was an exact match to Jesse's sister Susan's great-grandson and great-great-grandson.

$57,475.00 WAS PAID for a wanted poster of Jesse James on June 23, 2012. The wanted poster did not feature a photo and did not say "Dead or Alive." Turns out the law wanted James very much alive to stand trial.

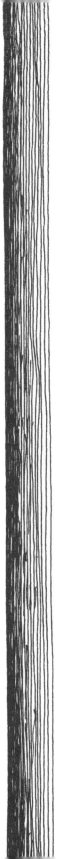

Jesse James was killed in his living room, and his wife, Zerelda, and their two young children, Mary and Jesse, were nearby in the kitchen.

VOCABULARY OF THE CIVIL WAR

- **Abolitionists:** people committed to ending slavery
- **Border States:** Delaware, Kentucky, Maryland, Missouri, and West Virginia; states located between Northern and Southern states
- **Bushwhacker:** Missourians who resisted and often ambushed the Union troops during the Civil War
- **Secessionists:** persons interested in Southern states becoming independent from the Union
- **Unionists:** Southerners who didn't want the Southern states to secede

BILLY THE KID

I WON'T GROW UP

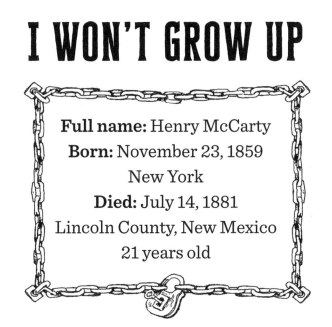

Full name: Henry McCarty
Born: November 23, 1859
New York
Died: July 14, 1881
Lincoln County, New Mexico
21 years old

Billy the Kid was a skinny stick of a person. His real name was Henry McCarty, but nobody cares about that. His youthful size made him an easy mark for bullies and con men, so he got good at charming his way out of jams. If that didn't work, he'd shoot his way out. He wasn't naturally bad; he just had no guidance about what he should be when he grew up. Billy never met his dad, and he literally stopped growing at fourteen when his mom died. From then on, there was no love, no guidance, no growth spurts. Family friends took him in, but it didn't last. His first crime was stealing butter. And the next thing everybody knew, he was stealing horses and shooting people. In record time, Billy the Kid went from most unwanted boy to the boy Most Wanted.

Without his mom around, Billy looked for love in all the wrong places. He needed a place to belong, so he joined a gang of little trouble- makers. The first time Billy was caught for stealing, the sheriff spanked him, even though fifteen was way past spanking age. The second time he was caught with sto- len goods, Billy was thrown in jail. But the guard underestimated the squirt's  smarts. Billy cajoled his way out of his cell so he could exercise in the hallway, and then the jailer left Billy alone. Billy escaped up and out the jailhouse chimney.

Jail time didn't scare Billy straight. Instead, he joined a gang of grown men who were big-time horse thieves and planned to use Billy's stealthy size to their advantage. It was dangerous, but Billy wanted to belong somewhere. Stealing a horse was like stealing someone's car today, but a lot worse—it was Grand Theft Seabiscuit. If you got caught, you were either shot on the spot or hanged. Be- cause he looked like a kid, Billy was caught and thrown in jail in- stead, which was a lucky break that led to another breakout. Even with iron shackles recently soldered on by a blacksmith, Billy used his Squirm-Out-of-Jail-Free card and escaped through a vent.

Billy's next bad decision was buying a gun and then finding some- one to shoot. Smart escapees wouldn't go play poker near the jail they just broke out of, but Billy did. Then his luck ran out. He ran into the shackle-maker/blacksmith who probably lost business with the newspaper report of Billy's escape. The blacksmith pushed the light-weight kid around, so Billy shot him dead. Billy stole a horse hitched out front and took off.

Now Billy's résumé included murderer, horse thief, and escape artist—he was seventeen. To elude capture, he changed his name to William Bonney.

This fooled no one.

Billy headed for the middle-of-nowhere Lincoln County, New Mexico. It was west of Where Is Everybody? and south of More Cows Than People, and in the heart of All Things Beige. There was one person for every fifteen square miles. If communing with cattle was his goal, he had picked the right place, but if Billy wanted to go clean, he had chosen the wrong stinking territory. The homicide rate in New Mexico was forty-seven times higher than the national aver-age. It was the Wild West. And it was extra wild after the Civil War. Every surviving soldier went home with a weapon, and America had

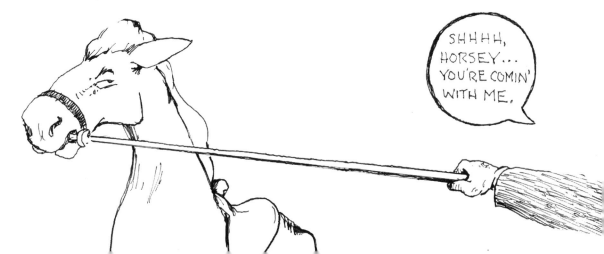

turned into a gun-toting, trigger-happy place. In Lincoln, it was second nature to shoot someone who bugged you. The last word in most minor disputes was a smoking six-shooter.

It wasn't a place a person wanted to stand out. But Billy was hard to ignore since he was able to say "stick 'em up" in Spanish and English *and* shoot you with his right or left hand. His giant sombrero provided shade and a bigger presence. And Billy could turn a girl's head with his brown curls, blue eyes, and squirrel-like front teeth. He was adorable. Women either wanted to be his mommy or his sweetheart.

When the Kid arrived in Lincoln County, ranchers were knocking themselves out to get control of the government contracts to supply food to Indian reservations and military posts. It sparked all-out guerrilla warfare. Billy was hired by one of the greedy ranchers and joined in the fight. There was no right side and there were no heroes. Billy shot the sheriff, and he also shot the deputy.

Now he added cop killer to his résumé.

Usually what happened in New Mexico stayed in New Mexico, but Billy's youthful murder spree equaled good reading material, and he was front-page news across the country. Billy had superstar charisma, but somebody had to stop him.

Enter the newly elected Sheriff Pat Garrett. Garrett eclipsed Billy the Kid at practically six and a half feet tall. They didn't see eye to eye in more ways than one.

Billy's adorableness had dimmed because he was too trigger-happy, so some locals told Garrett where Billy and his gang were staying. Garrett and his posse surrounded Billy's little hideout.

At dawn, a sombrero-wearing outlaw opened the hideout door. It was the kind of hat Billy always wore—but not that time. Garrett shot the wrong man. Another gang member ran out, untied a horse, and tried to get it inside the building. Garrett shot the horse. Now there was one dead two-thousand-pound problem clogging up the doorway and the escape route out of there.

Billy couldn't find a way to flee this time and had to surrender.

It was Christmas Eve. It wasn't wrapped, but Billy got an iron bracelet/shackle with a connecting chain and matching anklets as an early Christmas present.

In a generous holiday mood, Garrett allowed Billy to visit his girlfriend, Paulita Maxwell, before heading out to his trial. Billy gave Paulita an impressive kiss while two armed guards enjoyed the show. Even on the wagon ride to where Billy was to face murder charges, he stayed in a good mood. "What's the use of looking on the gloomy side of everything?" he said.

But there was no bright side to the sentence of "hanged by the neck until his body be dead."

Seven armed guards took the shackled Billy to the Lincoln County jail. The execution date was twenty-two days away. That was an eternity to keep an escape artist like Billy the Kid on the premises.

Two deputies watched him day and night—except during mealtime, when one deputy took the other five prisoners over to the hotel to eat. While they were gone one night, Billy requested a trip to the outside toilet. The remaining deputy took the shackled Billy, clanking and hopping, to the privy. But when they returned to the jail, Billy whacked the deputy with his handcuffs, took his gun, and killed him. When the other deputy ran back to the jail, Billy shot him too.

Then Billy removed his shackles and took off on a horse.

Months went by and everybody figured any smart fugitive would have been long gone, but rumor had it Billy was with Paulita Maxwell at her family's ranch.

Garrett and two deputies headed to the Maxwell compound.

Around midnight, when the lights were out, Garrett went inside the house while his two deputies stayed on the porch.

Garrett snuck into Paulita's brother Pete's bedroom to ask about Billy.

Meanwhile, Billy wandered out to the porch with a butcher knife. He headed for a freshly slaughtered piece of meat hanging on a beam outside for a snack. Billy spotted the men in the dark, but he couldn't see who they were. In Spanish, Billy asked, *"¿Quién es?"* "Who is it?"

The deputies didn't answer.

Billy backed into the house and into Pete's bedroom and asked, "Pete, who are those men outside?" It was pitch-black; Billy didn't see Garrett sitting right there in the bedroom. Pete didn't want his family shot to pieces. It was time to give Billy up.

"It's him," Pete whispered to Garrett.

Garrett shot Billy twice.

Billy was dead. The twenty-one-year-old didn't get away that time. A person can survive only so many bad decisions, and Billy the Kid had reached his limit.

Some people never learn.

BILLY THE KID FACTS AND STATS

500-DOLLAR reward notice for Billy the Kid was printed in the *Las Vegas Gazette* in 1880. There was never a wanted poster for Billy the Kid.

> *I will pay $500 reward to any person or persons*
> *Who will capture William Bonny, alias The Kid, and*
> *Deliver him to any sheriff of New Mexico.*
> *Satisfactory proofs of identity will be required.*
> (Bonney was misspelled in the original notice.)

9 OUTLAWS besides Billy the Kid who were also known as "Kid": ("Kid" was a common nickname for young people who were handy with guns.)

Ace-High Kid
Apache Kid
Dutch Kid
Jimmy the Kid
Pecos Kid

Pockmarked Kid
Texas Kid
Verdigris Kid
Willie the Kid

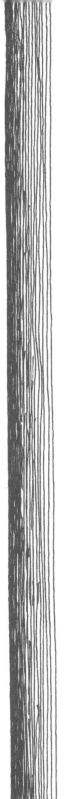

2 HOURS after Billy's death, the bullet hole in his chest finally started to bleed.

A rag was stuffed into the exit hole in his back, and one of Pete Maxwell's large white shirts was pinned to fit Billy so he could be properly dressed for his burial.

7 MONTHS before Billy's death, December 3, 1880, the name Billy the Kid was used for the first time in an article by J. H. Koogler for the *Las Vegas Gazette.* Putting "the" between "Billy" and "Kid" made it surprisingly hard to forget.

27 YEARS after Sheriff Pat Garrett killed Billy the Kid, Garrett met the same fate. Garrett was shot in the back of the head while he was urinating at the side of the road, by Wayne Brazil, who was angry about a land dispute.

2015 WAS THE YEAR that New Mexico created a death certificate for Billy the Kid. There had been many Billy the Kid impostors, and this finally put an end to rumors that he had survived.

$2.3 MILLION was paid for the only known photograph of Billy the Kid at the Old West Show & Auction in 2011.

SLANG OF THE WILD WEST

- **Ace in the Hole:** hideout or a hidden gun
- **Badlands:** barren, inhospitable land usually in western locations
- **Big Guns:** important people
- **Biscuit Shooter:** cook
- **Bone Orchard:** cemetery
- **Buckaroo:** cowboy or cowgirl
- **Make Tracks:** leave or walk away

 Billy the Kid's headstone has been stolen many times. His grave is now enclosed in a cage to protect it from theft and vandalism. No escape for Billy this time.

MATA HARI

I SPY A BAD GIRL

Real Name: Margaretha
Geertruida Zelle
Born: August 7, 1876
Leeuwarden, Holland
Died: October 15, 1917
Vincennes, France
41 years old

Mata Hari wasn't really a bad girl, but in the mind of the firing squad, she was. That's because in 1917, during World War I, the French had "spy fever." People were on the lookout for suspicious foreigners, and if you're looking hard enough to find something, you'll see it everywhere because you want it so much. Mata Hari was close enough to the spy profile to get caught in a trap of liars and women-haters. They called her the greatest woman spy of the century, even though there was nothing spylike about her. Her approach to world problems was to pretend they didn't exist. All she had done was to become the boss of her own body, which unfortunately didn't last long, because society made women like Mata Hari—who didn't follow the rules—pay.

Before Mata Hari was Mata Hari she was Margaretha Zelle, born in 1876 in the Netherlands. She was one of four children, and the only girl. Her family was wealthy until her dad made some bad investments and went bankrupt. When she was thirteen, her dad left in search of work and never came back.

A year later, Margaretha's mom died. Her twin brothers were sent to live with Dad in Amsterdam. Her other brother went to live with her mom's family, but nobody picked Margaretha to live with them. Abandoned and orphaned, Margaretha was taken in reluctantly by her godfather. Knowing that girls from poor families rarely got married, her godfather signed her up at a vocational boarding school to learn a skill.

Except her training was cut short when the principal inappropriately touched her where it wasn't okay. There's no way it was her fault—she was the victim—but Margaretha was blamed anyway. In today's world that principal would be arrested, but back then everything was stacked against women. Margaretha was kicked out

of school. Feeling ashamed of Margaretha, her godfather kicked her out of his house too.

Without options, Margaretha answered a newspaper ad. *Officer on home leave from Dutch East Indies would like to meet a girl of pleasant character—object matrimony.* Margaretha was broke, but she spoke five languages, and she was cute—so she sent a photo. No one had ever thought of doing that before.

Captain Rudolf MacLeod did not send a photo because he was grumpy-looking and twice her age. But penniless girls couldn't be picky. Rudolf's uncle had to approve of Margaretha before Rudolf could marry. She's "young," the uncle admitted, "but good-looking." As a matter of fact, she was darn good-looking. It was a match.

The youthful Margaretha had a son and a daughter as she followed Rudolf while he served in locations like Java, Tupang, and Sumatra— places where men outnumbered women two to one—which meant a large chunk of the population couldn't keep their eyes off her. This enraged Captain Rudolf, and he ended up being a scary, mean drunk. He beat her, spit on her, and taunted her with a loaded gun, saying he could shoot her and no one would know.

Margaretha lived in fear. It didn't seem possible, but things got even worse and the unimaginable happened. Her two-year-old son died after a short illness, and then Rudolf kidnapped their daughter. Margaretha filed for divorce. She courageously shared all the abuse she had endured, but she lost custody of her daughter because that's what happened when a woman rocked the boat back then. The world wasn't a fair or safe place for women.

But something clicked.

The beaten-down, twenty-eight-year-old Margaretha didn't want to be the victim any longer. She took control of her life. Starting from scratch, she rebooted with a name change: Mata Hari. She moved to Paris and rebranded herself as a dancer. She made up a routine of "sacred dances" to the gods, Bollywood style, with undulating moves she had picked up in the Indies, and she charged admission. She knew men's weak spot, and it became her sweet spot. She said goodbye to the hard life at the mercy of men. It was time to cash in on her good looks and rule her own destiny.

The pointy Javanese headdress, beaded metallic bra, and sheer clothes she wore added authenticity as she swooped her arms around and showed off her ankle jewelry. Despite wearing earrings the size of small chandeliers, she classed up a basically trashy routine by concocting stories behind her dances, which she explained in French, Dutch, German, English, and Malay.

Her old life wasn't worth remembering, so she made up a pretend past, and Mata Hari rocked it. She'd say that she was born in Java, or that her temple-dancer mother died giving birth to her. This worked because it was about ninety years before the truth was just a Google search away.

She became a world-famous dancer and went on a tour to Russia, Spain, The Hague, Monte Carlo, Milan, and Sicily—and she was paid a lot of money to do it.

Fancy clothes, jewels, and rooms in high-class hotels kept her in style, and after her shows, she picked who she'd spend time with one on one. Her favorite companions were military personnel, politicians, and police chiefs from all over the world.

But by 1914, World War I had started and women were expected to be dutiful homemakers. She had tried that; it didn't work for her. Depending on which side of the war they were on, spectators saw Mata Hari as always dancing or hanging out with the enemy.

Being a foreigner, she was under suspicion wherever she went. She had to cancel her dancing gig in Germany because she kept getting arrested. And then her German talent agent stole her clothes and jewels, worth about $250,000 today. She was furious. That was

ten years of her hard-earned money! After that, it was a no-brainer to say yes when she was offered money ($61,000 in today's money) to become a German spy. To her, the money was just partial payback for her stolen property, but she had no intention of doing any real spying for the Germans.

She went back to Paris and had special friends there too. She was a foreigner—the French had their own bad case of "spy fever," so a traveling showgirl like Mata Hari had to be watched. Two French inspectors began spying on her, and they interrogated everyone she knew.

She contacted Captain George Ladoux, the head of French Intelligence, to find out why her once-friendly companions weren't calling anymore.

Ladoux had hired the two inspectors because he suspected Mata Hari was a spy, but he hadn't found any evidence after almost a year of searching. So he set a trap to get her. He asked her to meet a high-ranking German officer and sweet-talk him into divulging military secrets that would help France.

She agreed to do it, but she was a lousy spy. There's only so much reinvention that one woman can do. First, she couldn't sneak around because she was a celebrity, and second, current events went in one ear and out the other. Her German captain mumbled something about a submarine landing in Morocco during their time together. It was just gossip, but it was espionage-worthy enough for her, and she called Ladoux to share what she'd learned.

On her return to Paris to collect her paycheck, not knowing she had been tricked, Mata Hari was surprised when she was arrested on February 13, 1916, and accused of being a German spy. Five inspectors raided her hotel room and took her in.

Pierre Bouchardon, nicknamed the Grand Inquisitor, interrogated her.

It had to be a mistake.

"Someone is playing with me," she said, and expected to go home. She didn't even bother calling her lawyer. But Bouchardon twisted her words as she explained she was working for Ladoux. Bouchardon locked her up in a padded cell in the damp, filthy, rat-infested Saint-Lazare prison. Her imprisonment was hidden from the public while Bouchardon put Mata Hari back in her place.

She was just Margaretha again, at the mercy of a hostile, oppressive man.

For five months, Margaretha practically lived in solitary confinement while Bouchardon badgered her until she had a nervous breakdown and she was coughing up blood. When she finally got a lawyer, he couldn't do anything to help her.

Fifty-three male friends of Mata Hari's were questioned. They all agreed they were with her for sweet talk, not war talk.

There wasn't any proof of her guilt, until out of the blue Ladoux produced some fake telegrams that incriminated her. And that was that.

Her trial records were kept secret. No one was allowed in the courtroom while she faced seven male military judges and a male prosecutor.

The prosecutor called her the greatest woman spy of the century. She was accused of killing 50,000 French men, which was more made up than her phony family history.

Mata Hari was judged on how she lived. She should have been applauded for making a life out of nothing except her desperate need to survive. But she was sentenced to death and shot by a firing squad instead.

The last twelve men she faced had loaded rifles ready to take her life. She blew a kiss to the firing squad before they shot her dead on October 15, 1917.

No one claimed her body. Her head was given to the Institute of Anatomy Museum in Paris for the study of criminals' skulls. Her innocent skull must have skewed their results.

She had been abandoned, molested, beaten, and deprived of her children. Against all odds, Mata Hari bravely turned her hopeless life around, but it didn't last. Bad men got their way in the end, and they wiped her right off the planet.

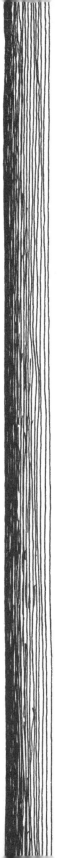

MATA HARI FACTS AND STATS

Mata Hari is a Malay phrase meaning "sunrise." *Mata* means "eye," and *Hari* means "day," and together they are "the eye of the day."

100 YEARS after Mata Hari's birth, a statue of her was erected in her birthplace, Leeuwarden, Holland.

4 DAYS after Mata Hari's execution, George Ladoux was arrested as a German spy. Four months later he was declared innocent.

500 PEOPLE were arrested and suspected of being spies by George Ladoux during World War I. Most of them were shot.

2 DECADES was about the time it took before both the investigator and the prosecutor in Mata Hari's case admitted they had no real evidence to convict her.

Investigator Pierre Bouchardon: "I still do not know what Mata Hari has done. In fact, nobody knows what Mata Hari has done!"

Prosecutor André Mornet: "Between you and me, there wasn't enough evidence to flog a cat."

4 YEARS OLD was the age of Jeanne Louise MacLeod the last time she was allowed to see her mom. Mata Hari tried many times to see her daughter, but her ex-husband wouldn't allow it.

2 YEARS after Mata Hari's death, Jeanne Louise MacLeod suddenly died. She was only twenty-one years old. The cause of death was a bleeding brain, either by a cerebral hemorrhage or aneurysm.

 Before Mata Hari was executed, she wrote a letter to her daughter. She gave the letter to her jailors to deliver, but the letter was never seen again.

SPY PRIMER

- **Espionage:** spying or using spies to gather information about the activities of a foreign government
- **Femme Fatale:** a woman who charms men with her looks and mystery; translated from French, it means "deadly woman"
- **Firing Squad:** a military unit assigned to carry out a death sentence by shooting
- **Scapegoat:** a person who is blamed for something he or she didn't do

TYPHOID MARY

DON'T EAT WHERE YOU POOP

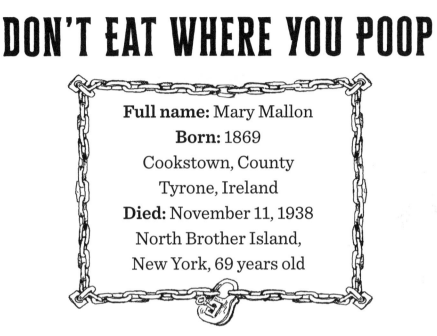

Full name: Mary Mallon
Born: 1869
Cookstown, County
Tyrone, Ireland
Died: November 11, 1938
North Brother Island,
New York, 69 years old

Mary Mallon went about her life denying the obvious. She made people sick. It didn't have to happen, but Mary didn't wash after going to the bathroom. People usually keep that dirty little secret to themselves. Except with secrets, you have to cover your tracks, and Mary always left a clue. She was a cook, and no matter what recipe Mary followed, there was one ingredient no one wanted but they got anyway: Mary's cooties, and they had a killer ingredient—typhoid. She didn't exactly mean to poison the food with a deadly disease . . . not at first, anyway.

But the poop was in the pudding.

At fifteen years old, Mary Mallon sailed to America to increase her chances of survival. She left Ireland, a country that lived on potatoes until they were all destroyed by a disease called blight not once but twice. A million people had died from starvation, and another three million were barely hanging on. Mary witnessed a lot of hardship. The New World had food. Mary, along with 1.5 million other Irish people, went to get some.

Immigrants had it hard, so Mary got tough. With her drive to never go hungry, Mary became a professional cook. Her work was sloppy, and her attitude brusque, but her food was tasty enough for her to be hired as a private chef for wealthy families. She ate her vegetables and grew into a self-sufficient, well-fed immigrant success story.

Others around her, though, seemed to be jinxed. Practically everywhere she worked, people got deathly ill. Of the last eight families Mary cooked for, seven families got typhoid. Mary must have noticed a trend, but she just packed up and moved on.

It happened again at each new job. She watched as the once healthy got fevers high enough to fry an egg on their forehead, icepick-between-the-eyes headaches, and a bellyache that killed all desire for food. As a matter of fact, it killed everybody's appetite, so over and over again, with fewer people to cook for, Mary kept moving to keep cooking.

Typhoid is spread hand to mouth. Basically, the poop germs of an infected person are swallowed. In 1907, more than six hundred people in New York had done just that and died from it, and Mary had cooked for a few of them. There was no hand sanitizer or moist toilettes, and a lot of people didn't even have a sink. But Mary had no excuse, because wherever she worked there was plumbing.

But not everyone had running water. Cities were one big health hazard, overrun with diseases, rodents, and rotting garbage. It was time to clean them up. Conditions were slowly being improved by the work of people like Dr. George Soper. He was an epidemiologist (germ finder), and he figured out the origin of typhoid outbreaks like a game of Clue. At one of Mary's jobs, six of the eleven people she was cooking for got sick, and Dr. Soper followed the long and winding fecal trail right to Mary. No one had blamed Mary before— she wasn't sick, so it couldn't have

been her. But Dr. Soper wasn't so sure. As she always did after an out-break, Mary had taken off, but no one knew where she'd gone.

Until there was another outbreak on Park Avenue in the home of the Bowen family, and the young daughter died. Dr. Soper showed up in person to solve the puzzle: It was Mary Mallon cooking in the kitchen with icky bathroom germs on her hands. She killed the girl. And to prove it, Dr. Soper asked Mary to poop and pee in a cup so he could take it to the lab and test it for typhoid.

Excuse me?

Mary expressed her shock and distaste for that idea at the top of her lungs. He had no right to come to her workplace and accuse her of killing someone. He'd get her fired, make her un-hirable, and who knows what else. She aimed a carving fork at Dr. Soper. If he didn't get lost, she'd kill him. Dr. Soper ran away at fork-point.

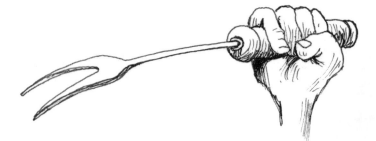

People had died around Mary her whole life—what's the big deal now? Besides, she was strong and healthy; that's why she *didn't* get sick. Couldn't he see that?

Dr. Soper only saw a health threat. Afraid of being gutted, Dr.

Soper secretly followed Mary home. He returned later with another doctor for backup. They ambushed Mary at home and asked again for her oh-so-personal samples. Mary vehemently was oh-so-NOT doing that. Both doctors ran for their lives.

Dr. Soper passed the job on to Dr. Sara Josephine Baker. Maybe Mary would be more willing to give her bodily fluids to a woman doctor (a rarity in those days).

After Mary slammed the door in Dr. Baker's face, Baker returned with five policemen. But Mary climbed out a window, ran across the yard, scaled a fence, and then got an accomplice to stack trash cans outside an outhouse (an outdoor bathroom) while Mary hid inside for three hours. Talk about germs. No one could find her until someone noticed Mary's clothing stuck in the door. It took all five policemen to get Mary into the horse-drawn ambulance. Dr. Baker sat on Mary the whole way to the hospital.

Dr. Soper finally got the bodily fluids he wanted and the proof he needed. He told Mary the inconvenient truth: she was the first healthy typhoid carrier to be found in the United States. "I will write a book about your case." They would both become famous. He would be the smart doctor, and Mary would be the woman with filthy habits.

No, Mary didn't want a book deal. And no, she didn't believe the lab tests. She had worked hard, followed all the rules, and found a way to fit in with the richest families. She had survived. If she was so sick, why did it take five policemen to subdue her? The two of them didn't agree about a single fact. Mary wasn't one to sit still and listen to Soper making up lies about how she had infected people. Mary went into the bathroom (again) and slammed the door.

Because Mary was as stubborn as a goat, they wouldn't let her go home. She was moved to North Brother Island, a twenty-acre whittled piece of earth in the middle of New York Harbor. That would show her. The only thing there was a hospital for the sick people nobody wanted around. It was a health prison. Mary was placed in a bungalow all alone.

She wasn't popular, and people talked behind her back. She got the nickname Typhoid Mary. People kept their distance, except for the doctors incessantly stopping by to collect her bowel movements. They also offered up different cures, but Mary wasn't interested. This went on for more than two years.

Mary's forced confinement was written about in the newspapers, and concerned readers donated money to help her. Mary got a lawyer and went to court.

But she still wasn't allowed to go home.

Finally, three years after being ripped away from her life, Mary was permitted to leave. There were now fifty documented healthy carriers identified in New York State, and Mary was the only one locked up. It wasn't fair.

To be released, Mary agreed to wash better, never prepare food for other people, show up for routine tests, and inform the Health Department of her address.

Mary said yes to all this, but she really meant no.

Mary disappeared and was back on the lam. Before the internet, security cameras, or monitoring ankle bracelets, there was no way to find her or to know if her cooties were going to be back on someone's dinner plate.

Five years later, at the Sloane Hospital for Women, a maternity hospital, twenty-five people got typhoid and two died. Those people had all eaten food from the dining hall (think school cafeteria). Everyone there had teased the cook, Mrs. Brown, by calling her Typhoid Mary. It was a sick joke . . . ha ha . . . eeow.

It *was* Typhoid Mary.

Mary Mallon had used the fake name Mrs. Brown to keep cooking. Interesting name choice for a person who wasn't washing her hands after going number two! Was it a twisted joke or a secret warning for those in the know? Whatever her thinking, denying the existence of germs, cooking for people when she shouldn't, and endangering pregnant women and babies—it couldn't get worse. She blew it. She was dirty *and* guilty. She was a human murder weapon and she didn't care.

The authorities chased Mary again. They followed her to a friend's house. Sergeant Coneally rang the doorbell, but no one answered. Coneally climbed a ladder to a second-floor window but was scared off by a barking bulldog. His next time up the ladder, he brought a hunk of meat to distract the dog, and then he found Mary hiding in the bathroom. Again. She was crouched down on the tile floor when he finally got the door open.

She spent the next twenty-three years back on North Brother Island. Near the end, she had so much junk piled up in her cottage, it was impossible to move around. Being a hoarder was another one of Mary's little secrets.

After a paralyzing stroke, she spent the last six years of her life in bed. It was impossible to wash herself even if she had wanted to.

Kitchen closed.

TYPHOID MARY FACTS AND STATS

TYPHOID FEVER SYMPTOMS:

- Diarrhea
- Fever
- Headache
- Loss of appetite
- Rash on stomach and chest
- Severe cramping
- Tenderness

10 to 30 percent of typhoid patients die if they go untreated. With antibiotics, the fatality rate is only 1 to 4 percent.

33 PEOPLE were infected with typhoid fever by Mary Mallon. Some places she worked kept no records, so most likely there were more.

3 PEOPLE DIED from catching Mary's typhoid.

4 FAMOUS TYPHOID FEVER VICTIMS in history who were NOT infected by Mary Mallon:

- Abigail Adams
- Alexander the Great
- Wilbur Wright
- Willie Lincoln

TYPHOID FEVER VS. TYPHUS:

Even though they sound alike, typhoid fever and typhus are two completely different diseases.

Typhoid fever is spread if you eat or drink the *Salmonella typhi* bacteria. The bacteria is carried in the stool of an infected person.

Typhus is spread by a flea, mite, lice, or tick bite. If the bite is scratched and the skin breaks opens, the *Rickettsia* bacteria can enter the bloodstream.

1st WOMAN to earn a doctorate in Public Health at New York University was Dr. Sara Josephine Baker. She helped identify and capture Mary Mallon.

1st DIRECTOR of the new Bureau of Child Hygiene in the United States was also Dr. Sara Josephine Baker. There, she set up programs for midwife training, safe hygiene, and preventive care. She gave milk to children in poor communities and created a school health program. Dr. Baker's father had died of typhoid fever when she was sixteen years old.

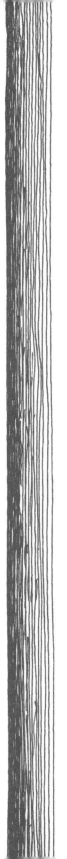

MARY MALLON'S SIGNATURE DISH:

Mary often served peaches and ice cream. Mary's dirty paws likely spread typhoid germs in this dessert and then into the mouths of others. Raw fruit and dairy products are perfect avenues for passing germs. The high temperatures of cooked foods are usually enough to kill the germs.

MARY'S STOOL STATS:

Laboratory proof showed that Mary Mallon remained a typhoid carrier while being incarcerated at North Brother Island.

DATES	TOTAL STOOL SAMPLES	POSITIVE	NEGATIVE
1907–1909	163	120	43
1915–1936	230	207	23

MARY MALLON'S MISSING FIVE YEARS:

Health authorities lost track of Mary Mallon for five years before they caught up with her at Sloane Hospital for Women. It's impossible to know whether Mary infected people during this time period.

CATCHY EPIDEMICS

- **Cholera:** A person can get cholera by drinking contaminated water or eating contaminated food. The source of the contamination is usually the feces of an infected person that gets into food and/or water.

- **Scarlet Fever:** These bacteria are spread when the infected person coughs or sneezes and the germ droplets get in the air. If you touch your mouth, nose, or eyes after touching something that has these droplets on it, you may become ill. If you drink from the same glass or eat from the same plate as the sick person, you could also become ill.

- **Smallpox:** Smallpox can be spread through direct contact with infected bodily fluids or contaminated objects such as bedding or clothing.

- **Tuberculosis (TB):** When a person with TB coughs and sneezes, droplets of bacteria get in the air and healthy people breathe these in and become infected.

- **Yellow Fever:** This disease is transmitted to humans by the bite of an infected mosquito.

RASPUTIN

SUPER CREEP

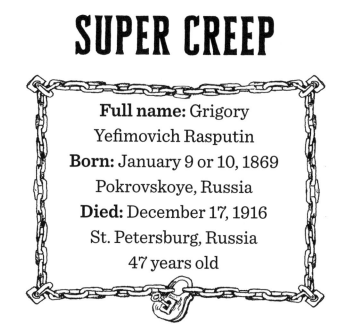

Full name: Grigory
Yefimovich Rasputin
Born: January 9 or 10, 1869
Pokrovskoye, Russia
Died: December 17, 1916
St. Petersburg, Russia
47 years old

Rasputin had a terrible reputation. In Russian, *Rasputin* means "good-for-nothing," and Grigory Rasputin lived up to it. Rasputin was born in Siberia, Russia, where people farmed, hunted, drank vodka, and went to church. Only 4 percent of the people could read, and Rasputin wasn't one of them. But he could hear, and he heard voices coming out of the sky. He decided it was God, and some people believed him. Less believable was his claim that he could predict the future and heal the sick. But once he convinced the right two people to believe that—the tsar of Russia, Nicholas II, and his overly religious and superstitious wife, Empress Alexandra—he was set for life (as long as it lasted). With their blessing, Rasputin went from creepy nobody to major player in the fall of the Russian Empire, but he was a hard guy to bring down.

Rasputin ended up in St. Petersburg, where he crafted his worship of God into a theatrical performance to be noticed, and to get ahead. While listening to sermons, he'd grimace, make crazy eyes at everyone, and bounce around on the pew. When he got the chance, he'd talk nonstop to anyone within earshot about his beliefs, and about how God had chosen him to do great things. He repelled many, but his big unblinking eyes mesmerized others, and before long, people were lining up to see him. He was odd, but the Russian Orthodox Church leaders didn't want Rasputin stealing their followers, so they embraced him and gave him the title of *starets* (person with special wisdom).

As a *starets,* Rasputin was able to wrangle an introduction to Tsar Nicholas II and Empress Alexandra of the Romanov Dynasty—and it was a match made in heaven.

Nicholas II had inherited the Russian Empire, with its massive problems and brewing revolution. He didn't want this job, and his answer to everything was "What am I going to do?" So his wife,

Alexandra, told Nicholas what to do. Meanwhile, she was moody and sat around fretting that something bad was about to happen. The two of them didn't have a clue what regular people were like, nor did they care. They had four daughters and a son, who was heir to the throne. But the heir had hemophilia, which meant he could bleed to death from the smallest scratch. Nicholas and Alexandra endlessly prayed for his health.

The tsar and his wife were easy marks for a guy trying to get ahead. Rasputin saw their weak spots and took aim. With his arms flapping and his eyes darting around, he told Alexandra not to worry about what *might* happen; he could predict the future, and he'd let her in on it. And since he could heal the sick, he'd keep her son alive. Then Rasputin told Nicholas that he'd get answers for him about managing Russia, because he had a shortcut to heaven and to God's advice.

With talk like that, Rasputin became a palace regular. Nicholas didn't make any decisions without Rasputin's blessing. And if the young heir had so much as a nosebleed, Rasputin got a call. Meanwhile, the tsar's children's nanny and their nurse complained that Rasputin wouldn't keep his hands off them. These allegations could have ruined Rasputin's church career. Instead, Alexandra fired the nurse and the nanny.

Outside the palace walls, Rasputin was drunk all the time and hanging out with different women every night. He'd say, "I love everybody," which was getting him into a lot of trouble.

The church leaders gave Rasputin a new title: fraud. Monthly bulletins described Rasputin's unholy activities, and a full report was given to the tsar.

Not thorough fact-checkers, Nicholas and Alexandra thought it was easier to just fire every church official and replace them with Rasputin's buddies.

The police and the prime minister put together their own dossiers of Rasputin's sinful behavior. Rasputin was literally dropping his pants in public. Nicholas and Alexandra refused to believe any of it. Their solution was to replace the chief of police, the assistant chief of police, and the prime minister with men that Rasputin suggested. Nicholas even outlawed writing about Rasputin in the newspapers.

Rasputin was a real creep, but Nicholas and Alexandra didn't think so, and what they said was the law, which showed the flaws in a system where monarchs have absolute power—especially when a monarch wasn't really up to the job. Dealing with their Rasputin problem was nothing compared to food shortages, angry mobs in the streets, and workers on strike, all of which they ignored.

Alexandra made clear in a letter to Nicholas, "Show to all, that you are the Master ... now comes your reign of will & power ... obedience they must be taught. ..."

And things got worse in 1914 when much of the world became engulfed in World War I. One year later, 1.5 million Russians were dead.

While Nicholas went off to take *pretend charge* of military operations of the war, Alexandra was left to run the government, and Rasputin was her wingman. Rasputin told her, "If I die or you desert me, you will lose your son and your crown." Rasputin had power over Alexandra, and she had power over the tsar.

It was the most politically corrupt time in Russia's history. Within eighteen months, there had been four different prime ministers, five ministers of the interior (police), and four ministers of agriculture. Unqualified candidates were being elevated to high office just because Rasputin liked them. Before long, everyone hated Rasputin, except two people. Rasputin got hate mail, he was beaten up, and a car rammed into his sleigh.

The wealthy Prince Felix Yusupov, who was married to Nicholas's niece Irina, decided to kill Rasputin since the police, the government, and the Church couldn't stop him. Felix easily found four other people happy to help him murder Rasputin.

Knowing the "holy man's" weakness for women, Felix lured Rasputin by pretending his beautiful wife, Irina, wanted to meet him. Since Felix's palace was across the street from a police station, they needed a quiet method of murder, so poison was their weapon of choice.

It was ten degrees below zero at midnight on December 16, 1917, when Felix picked up Rasputin. During the day, Rasputin had downed about twelve bottles of wine, so it was no surprise when he stumbled getting into Felix's car.

If Rasputin could predict the future, he missed what was about to happen next.

At Felix's palace, potassium cyanide had been sprinkled in six little cream cakes and in the wine. Felix took Rasputin in the back door of his palace, which led to a winding staircase to the basement. Felix had dolled it up to look like a fancy dining room with gold bowls, ivory carvings, and a polar-bear-skin rug. Felix told Rasputin that unexpected guests had shown up (not really) so they couldn't go upstairs and see Irina just yet. As they waited for the fake guests to leave, Rasputin ate the poisoned cakes and drank the poisoned wine while the other four conspirators stayed hidden just up the stairs.

To kill time while the poison kicked in, Felix grabbed the guitar in the corner and started singing . . . and singing . . . and singing.

Two hours later, Rasputin still wasn't dead. Felix excused himself and went upstairs.

After a short huddle with the other guys about what to do next, Felix grabbed a gun, went back down to Rasputin, and shot him in the chest. Rasputin collapsed on the polar bear rug. The other guys hurried down and saw a dead Rasputin. His blood was getting all over the white rug, so they dragged his body off it.

The schemers went upstairs to have a cigar. When Felix went down to check the body, Rasputin opened his eyes, stood up, and grabbed Felix. Felix wriggled free, and Rasputin ran out into the courtyard. One of the other guys, Purishkevich, grabbed a gun and ran after Rasputin. Two shots missed, but the third shot hit Rasputin in the back. With Rasputin splayed out on the ground, Purishkevich shot Rasputin in the forehead and then kicked him in the temple.

Two police officers from across the street heard the gunshots and came over. So proud of what he had done to save Russia, Purishkevich blurted out, "I killed Grigory Rasputin!" Luckily, the police officers hated Rasputin too, and they just helped drag Rasputin's body back inside the palace.

Felix was freaking out and he didn't want to take any chances that Rasputin might wake up again, so he took a two-pound dumbbell and whacked Rasputin in the head with it.

This was so far from Felix's normal behavior, he passed out cold.

The other guys wrapped Rasputin's legs in his fur coat, rolled the body in a dark blue curtain, tied it with rope, and then threw the bundled body in the car.

They drove to the Great Petrovsky Bridge. The Neva River was frozen solid, except for a hole the killers had scoped out earlier that day.

The assassins aimed Rasputin's limp corpse above the hole and dropped it over the railing. They heard a splash. They'd forgotten to tie the weights on the body so it would sink.

The next day, rumors started to spread that Rasputin was dead. People spontaneously started singing the national anthem, and strangers hugged each other. A few days later, Rasputin's frozen body was fished out of the water.

Three months after Rasputin was killed, Tsar Nicholas II was forced to give up the throne.

In reality, the only special ability Rasputin had was to get what he wanted. Rasputin used religion and his position of trust to take advantage of people. Nicholas and Alexandra had a lot of power, but no answers, and they desperately needed to believe that Rasputin knew more than they did. But looking for and hoping there's something other than reality to solve your problems makes a person a perfect target for a con man like Rasputin.

RASPUTIN FACTS AND STATS

EMPRESS ALEXANDRA ROMANOV planned Rasputin's funeral, and she prevented Rasputin's wife and two daughters from attending.

5 MEN murdered Rasputin:

- Prince Felix Yusupov
- Grand Duke Dimitri Pavlovich
- Lieutenant Sergei Sukhotin
- Vladimir Purishkevich
- Dr. Stanislaw Lazavert

No one was ever charged with the crime.

250 YARDS is the distance Rasputin's body floated away from the bridge where it had been dropped. It was frozen into an odd position and it couldn't fit in the coffin, so the body was loaded into a large wood crate and taken to a chapel to thaw out.

4 HOURS was about the time it took Dmitry Kosorotov to do Rasputin's autopsy. It was performed at Chesmensky Hospital. The police had forced Kosorotov to do it late at night because officials wanted to keep it a secret.

7 FINDINGS in Rasputin's autopsy:

- Body reeked of alcohol, indicating Rasputin was drunk when he died
- Clothes covered in blood
- Blackened right eye
- Nose crushed
- One bullet went through his left chest.
- Second bullet passed through his right kidney in his lower back.
- Third bullet went into his forehead—this bullet killed him instantly.

Rasputin's autopsy reports disappeared after the Russian Revolution.

1918 WAS THE YEAR Nicholas II's and Alexandra Romanov's lives took a tragic turn. The Bolsheviks ended their lives, along with their five children's.

- Olga: 22 years old
- Tatiana: 21 years old
- Maria: 19 years old
- Anastasia: 17 years (see chapter on Anna Anderson)
- Alexei: 13 years old

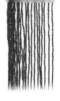

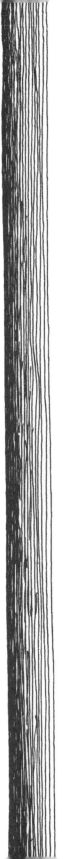

FYI RASPUTIN AND THE MOVIES

Prince Felix Yusupov sued the movie company MGM after it made *Rasputin and the Empress.* The prince was outspoken about his role in Rasputin's death, but he claimed the movie defamed his wife. The courts agreed, and the prince's wife was awarded a ton of money. You can thank Rasputin if you ever see this at the movies: "This is a work of fiction. Any similarity to actual persons, living or dead, or actual events, is purely coincidental."

RUSSIA FOR THE RECORD

- **Bolsheviks:** Led by Lenin, this political party took control of the Russian government after the revolution.
- **Hemophilia:** Bleeding disorder caused by the blood's inability to coagulate (stick together). Nicholas and Alexandra's only son and heir to the throne, Alexei, had hemophilia. The tsar and the tsarina hoped that Rasputin could cure Alexei. Hemophilia is incurable.
- **Romanov Family:** dynasty of Russian rulers from 1613 until 1917
- **Russian Revolution (1917):** Dissatisfied Russian people overthrew the imperial government because of scarcity of food, corrupt government, and an inept tsar.
- **Siberia:** an enormous region of Russia, about 5,207,900 square miles
- **Tsar:** highest ruler of Russia, derived from the Latin word *Caesar*
- **Tsarina:** tsar's wife, also called Empress

VINCENZO PERUGGIA

THE INVISIBLE MAN

Born: October 8, 1881
Dumenza, Italy
Died: October 8, 1925
Haute-Savoie, France
44 years old

You probably never heard of Vincenzo Peruggia. He committed an unthinkable crime, and then he was promptly forgotten. He didn't get a catchy nickname like Billy the Kid, and there are no legends about his life. Vincenzo Peruggia stole Leonardo da Vinci's *Mona Lisa* from the Louvre Museum in Paris, and he didn't even go to jail for it. It was easy too, because *Mona* was just hanging there on a nail. Back in 1911 the security at the Louvre was laissez-faire, which is French for "loosey-goosey." There were no surveillance cameras, motion detectors, or alarmed windows. The guards were a bunch of barely breathing old men, and there were a hundred passkeys floating around that opened every gallery, closet, vault, and stairwell.

The only thing protecting *Mona Lisa* was her newly made three-dimensional glass frame.

Mona Lisa was the first painting to get a glass-covered frame at the Louvre, and the young Italian Vincenzo Peruggia beat out some local Frenchmen for the job. Peruggia was skilled in carpentry and glasswork and had traveled far from home to find steady work. The French didn't like an Italian taking their jobs, so they hid Peruggia's tools, salted his food, and called him Macaroni, which may sound tasty but was meant as an insult. Peruggia didn't like them either, and he thought putting glass between the painting done by fellow Italian Leonardo da Vinci and the rude French people was a good thing. He hated that the French got to say *bonjour* to the *Mona Lisa* instead of the Italians back home. Peruggia decided to do something about it, *s'il vous plaît*.

On Sunday, August 20, 1911, Peruggia visited the Louvre, and when everybody left, he snuck inside a closet. Hiding in the Louvre was simple because it has one thousand rooms, including one that is four football fields long, and there was no security. Kicking back, Peruggia had a little Italian *vino* and *formaggio* picnic and went *buonanotte* in the closet.

Only maintenance workers were allowed in on Mondays. So the next morning, wearing his Louvre-issued white smock uniform, he emerged from the closet. The smock gave Peruggia carte blanche, meaning he could go anywhere in the museum, and he went right for *Mona Lisa*. Using just about every muscle in his five-foot, three-inch body, he lifted the seventy-seven pounds of *Mona Lisa* and her frame off the wall and carried her into a stairwell.

He unscrewed her clunky frame (that he had made) with a screwdriver. Unable to roll her up because she was painted on wood, Peruggia stuck *Mona Lisa* under his smock in the back. But the key he'd grabbed didn't work on the exit door, so he removed the doorknob with his screwdriver and was in the process of wrenching the lock off when a plumber came down the stairs.

Thinking fast, Peruggia hollered about the jammed door, making enough of a stink that the plumber didn't seem to mind that Peruggia was taking the door apart. Nor did the plumber notice there was a thirty-one-inch-tall painting stuck in back of the sixty-three-inch-tall Peruggia.

The plumber let him out the mangled door as if nothing were amiss. Once in the street, Peruggia wrapped *Mona Lisa* in his smock and headed home with the four-hundred-year-old masterpiece.

Even though *Mona Lisa* had been in the same spot at the Louvre for the last one hundred years, the empty space on the wall didn't cause alarm for the whole day. It took until Tuesday for anyone to realize *Mona Lisa* had left the building. In a matter of hours, the entire country of France went on lockdown.

Meanwhile, *Mona Lisa* was having her coming-out party. As fate would have it, the first photograph of her was taken just days before she was stolen. Newspapers across the globe printed her photo, and millions of people got to see her for the first time. Her disappearance had made her a celebrity, and it sparked an international dragnet to find her. Little did everyone know she was holed up in a one-room apartment only two miles from the Louvre.

Mona Lisa's previous digs had been a little more royal. Leonardo da Vinci never let her go until he died. After that, she spent fifty years in France's Francois I's bathroom. Then she moved on up to the bedrooms of Louis XIV, and finally Napoléon, before residing at the Louvre. Now *Mona Lisa*'s painted mug was in the not-royal-at-all Vincenzo Peruggia's one-room apartment, with his bed right next to the stove.

Forensic detective Alphonse Bertillon was hired to find the most famous mug shot in the world. After all, he invented the mug shot, and he was the first detective to win a murder case on the evidence of fingerprints. Bertillon found a thumbprint on *Mona Lisa*'s discarded frame. He got to work searching for a match in his criminal records.

Bertillon questioned all the museum employees. Peruggia lied about where he was on the morning of the crime, and no one checked his alibi. A detective searched Peruggia's room, but apparently not that well, because *Mona Lisa* was IN THERE. For some reason, Peruggia wasn't fingerprinted, unlike everyone else at the museum. Bertillon even had access to a full criminal profile on him, complete with mug shots and fingerprints because Peruggia had been arrested twice, once for attempted robbery and once for weapons possession.

The Italian practically had a target on him. But Bertillon still didn't spot him.

The plumber could have nailed him, but he didn't remember anything distinctive about the man he let out the door, like the fact that he was very short, had a huge handlebar mustache, and spoke with an Italian accent.

The plumber even looked through Bertillon's books of mug shots, but Peruggia's face wasn't ringing any bells for the plumber. Bells should have been ringing like crazy for *everyone*. If the French had been paying attention, *le jackpot* was right there, but it looked like Peruggia had the makings of the Invisible Man.

Two years went by, and *Mona Lisa*'s trail went cold. Peruggia could have kept *Mona Lisa* for the rest of his life. But then Peruggia answered an ad requesting art for sale, and he sent a letter to Alfredo Geri, an art dealer in Florence, Italy.

> *The stolen work of Leonardo da Vinci is in my possession.*
> *It seems to belong to Italy since its painter was an Italian.*

Intrigued, Geri set up a meeting.

Peruggia pulled another *coup* when he transported *Mona Lisa* across the border from France to Italy in a hidden compartment of a wooden box.

In case the guy with the stolen painting was a weirdo, and to help verify it as a real Leonardo painting, Geri brought along the director of the Uffizi Gallery in Florence, Italy, to the letter-writer's hotel room.

When they met, Peruggia asked for 500,000 lire ($2.14 million today), but added, "I did not take the picture through a desire for gain. . . ." The *Mona Lisa* was in fine shape; she only had a smudge on her cheek and a scratch on her left shoulder. Peruggia let the two men take the *Mona Lisa* to the Uffizi. Then they called the police.

Peruggia was arrested.

The Italians were crazed with joy to have *Mona Lisa* back where she belonged, in Italy. Even though the art thief Peruggia was put in jail, everyone thought he was a hero.

The *Mona Lisa* stayed in Italy for two weeks, and hundreds of thousands of people came to see her before she was taken by police guard back to France. The French were so embarrassed by this fiasco they didn't even prosecute Peruggia for the crime.

Peruggia went to trial in Italy, though. He was found guilty, but no one wanted him punished. He received a sentence of one year and fifteen days in prison, but since he had already been in jail for seven months during the trial, the judge decided that was long enough. Peruggia was released immediately.

And Vincenzo Peruggia's fifteen minutes of fame were over.

Mona Lisa's fame was just getting started. Before the theft, she had just been a local celebrity. But when Peruggia stole the *Mona Lisa,* he made her the most famous painting in the world.

Vincenzo Peruggia got no credit for that either.

VINCENZO PERUGGIA
FACTS AND STATS

ART CRIME:

Even today, with security cameras, motion detectors, bulletproof glass, alarmed windows, and guards watching your every move, art is often stolen from museums.

80 percent of all art heists are inside jobs.

5 ARTISTIC art heists:

1. In Italy, thieves hoisted a Gustav Klimt painting through a skylight from the Ricci Oddi Gallery.

2. A thief replaced a Henri Matisse painting with a forgery at Venezuela's Museo de Arte Contemporáneo de Caracas Sofía Imber (MACCSI). Nobody noticed for months.

3. Two men at Drumlanrig Castle in Scotland stole a da Vinci painting by pretending they were police officers.

4. Thieves in Stockholm took two Renoirs and a Rembrandt from the Nationalmuseum, and they got away in a speedboat.

5. A man in Paraguay dug an 80-foot tunnel from his shop to the National Museum of Fine Arts, and then he and his accomplices stole $1 million in art.

FBI ART CRIME TEAM:
16 SPECIAL AGENTS make up the FBI Art Crime Team (founded in 2004). It works worldwide in cooperation with foreign law enforcement.

14,850 STOLEN ARTWORKS worth over $165 million have been recovered.

BILLIONS OF DOLLARS' worth of art is stolen every year.

1 MONTH before the *Mona Lisa* was stolen, the Louvre hired a photographer to take photos of the painting, front and back. When the *Mona Lisa* was returned, authorities compared it with the photographs, which proved it was the real painting and not a fake.

THE BERTILLON SYSTEM OF CRIMINAL IDENTIFICATION:
Before mug shots, fingerprinting, DNA, and other forensic tools, one of the first systems of criminal identification was with body measurements. Alphonse Bertillon worked for the Paris police, copying descriptions of criminals onto index cards. His criminal identification method was called the **Bertillon system.**

This system focused on collecting detailed body measurements

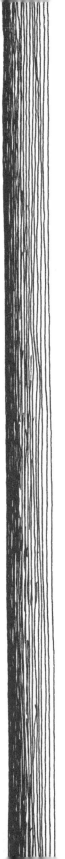

of criminals. It is one of the earliest scientific methods used in criminal investigations.

1 IN 4 MILLION: the chance that two people would have eleven body measurements all in common (height, weight, head circumference, shoe size, etc.)

1 IN 16: the chance that two people would have two measurements in common

BERTILLON BEGAN ADDING PHOTOS TO HIS INDEX CARDS—one of the face from the front and another from the side.
    The file cards became known as **portraits parlé** ("speaking portraits") in France. In the United States they became known as **mug shots,** referring to the photos of the face.

1900 WAS THE YEAR Bertillon began adding **fingerprints** to his criminal ID cards.

1 IN 64,000,000,000 (64 billion!): the chance of two people having the same fingerprint

HISTORY OF FINGERPRINTING (DACTYLOSCOPY):

- **1880:** Dr. Henry Faulds figured out you could use fingerprints to establish identity.
- **1897:** India was using fingerprinting to identify criminals.
- **1910:** Fingerprint evidence was first used successfully in the United States in an Illinois murder trial.
- **1924:** FBI set up a storehouse for fingerprint cards, and eventually had more than 200 million cards.
- **1991:** Automated Fingerprint Identification System (AFIS), a digital database, was created by the FBI.
- **1999:** To enlarge the scope and usage of AFIS, it was turned into the Integrated Automated Fingerprint Identification System (IAFIS), which stores, compares, and shares information with law enforcement agencies.

FYI **ALPHONSE BERTILLON** mistakenly compared the left thumbprint on *Mona Lisa*'s glass box to Vincenzo Peruggia's right thumbprint in his files. Every finger has a unique fingerprint.

LANGUAGE OF ART CRIMES

- **Art Forgery:** copied piece of art that is sold as if it were created by the original artist
- **Artnapping:** when a stolen piece of art is held for ransom
- **Black Market:** illegal market for stolen goods
- **Cultural Property:** art of cultural significance to a particular country or people
- **Fence:** someone who knowingly buys stolen items in order to sell them
- **Heist:** a robbery
- **Looting:** stealing of valuable goods from the enemy or captured city

BERNARD OTTO KUEHN

SECRET AGENT MAN

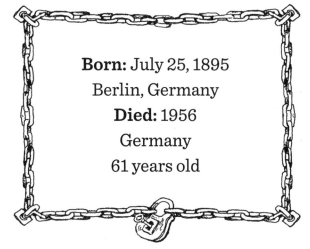

Born: July 25, 1895
Berlin, Germany
Died: 1956
Germany
61 years old

Bernard Otto Kuehn, known as Otto, went from being a lemonade salesman to Nazi informant to secret spy for the Japanese. He double-crossed friends and countries and he played a part in the bombing of Pearl Harbor on December 7, 1941, but no one figured out what Otto Kuehn was up to in time to stop him. He slithered under the radar of the FBI, U.S. Naval Intelligence, the War Department, and the World War II code-breakers. Hardly anyone knows Otto Kuehn's story even though what he was mixed up in killed a lot of people and prompted the United States to enter WWII. He was a slippery man in life, and in death.

Otto Kuehn gets credit for being a guy willing to try anything, but he was inclined to be average. He was born in Germany and at eighteen joined the German navy during World War I. His ship sank. He didn't drown, but he quit the navy. He studied architecture for a while but quit that to rejoin the navy. But the navy decided Kuehn was *not* navy material and kicked him out. He studied medicine, but that too was added to the growing list of dead-end experiences that weren't his thing.

But when Kuehn married—hitching his wagon to Friedel Birk and her two kids—Susie Ruth and Leopold, Kuehn got serious about a career.

Using inheritance money, Kuehn bought a sail freighter for shipping merchandise, but it crashed into a reef. Then his sparkling water and lemonade business failed too. He was a floor manager at a machinery shop, followed by flash-in-the-pan moments as a dairy inspector and a coffee importer. He was dead weight on surf and turf.

By 1935, pushing forty, the sun was setting on Kuehn's career horizon. He was in search mode for the next place to hitch his wagon when he attended a Nazi rally. Kuehn immediately signed on the dotted line.

This average-man-among-men became a Nazi informant in a German town. Kuehn got all buddy-buddy with people, and then he'd squeal on the ones that weren't Nazis. He had a skill after all—treating people like chewing gum on the bottom of his shoes. But when Kuehn squealed on the chief of police (who was a Nazi) for acting in a way that Kuehn didn't like, Kuehn was fired.

Kuehn wasn't even Nazi material.

On the other hand, members of his family were big-time Nazis. His wife worked in the Nazi welfare department; his stepson, Leopold, worked for the Nazi's public relations minister Joseph Goebbels; and his stepdaughter, Susie Ruth, was Goebbels's mistress. Kuehn's stepkids got Dad his next job—in espionage. The Nazis and the Japanese were teaming up against the United States, and there was a job opening for a sneaky, indistinguishable man willing to do anything—skills listed on Kuehn's resume.

Otto Kuehn headed to Hawaii via a short stop in Japan to get his secret-sleeper spy instructions from the Imperial Japanese Government. He was to slime his way into the U.S. Naval community at Pearl Harbor, snoop, take notes, and "wake up" when needed. Only if absolutely necessary would his "sleeper employers" send him money, because money could be traced. And to avoid suspicion, Kuehn was advised to get a regular job on the side. Kuehn was back to searching for a job.

His wife, two young sons, and stepdaughter joined Kuehn in Hawaii. Kuehn bought two houses with front-row views of U.S. Naval operations. He threw parties and got chummy with submarine personnel, battleship lieutenants, artillery workers, and commanders of the Naval Air Station. There was no resisting a man in uniform, and those men were everywhere, because sixty percent of the U.S. fleet (seventy warships) was at Pearl Harbor, including submarines, battleships, aircraft carriers, destroyers, patrol bombers, not to mention four hundred airplanes.

But just like always, Kuehn couldn't keep a steady job; he was going to blow his cover. He failed at the Modern Steel Furniture Company, Honolulu Iron Works, and never even made the cut to be a Fuller Brush salesman. It was looking like Otto Kuehn was about to add sleeper spy to his past employment history.

With no apparent source of income, the Kuehns were being watched by the Office of Naval Intelligence, and the FBI watched the Kuehns as well because their reason for being in Hawaii was deemed "mysterious." Even though they didn't want to, his sleeper-spy employers had to send him money. Payments to Kuehn were traced from Germany, Amsterdam, Holland, and Japan. The FBI also noticed that Kuehn's ten-year-old son dressed in a little sailor suit and got private  tours on battleships in restricted areas, and that Kuehn's wife and daughter's hair salon catered to navy officers' wives. And Kuehn installed a curious-looking dormer window in his attic.

Even so, after a year and a half, on November 24, 1941, the FBI concluded Otto Kuehn was a man capable of nothing much. "Activity of Kuehns fails to indicate they are engaged in espionage. . . ." Just being his wishy-washy self was great cover for what he was secretly working on. His skill set of so-so-ishness and mediocrity camouflaged his dark side. Kuehn's deep moral weakness must have completely escaped the FBI, because they also approved a date for Kuehn's U.S. citizenship.

Days later Kuehn got "wake up" instructions from the Japanese consulate. For $14,000 cash, with his son in tow, Kuehn went to Pearl Harbor and wrote down the strength and locations of each American ship at anchor and passed it to another Japanese spy. Kuehn designed a set of signals that he would use to send up-to-date information on U.S. fleet movements to the Japanese midget submarines hiding nearby out in the ocean.

Kuehn's proposed signals were a jamble of sheets on a clothesline, window lights (hence his new attic window), car headlights, and a ship with a star on the sail. He also hid clues in dictionaries and in want ads for beauty operators and for Chinese rugs for sale. He even had a secret post office box for "Jimmie," and if necessary, he'd set up hilltop brushfires. Every hour on the hour the signals would change, adding up to a whole kit and caboodle of incomprehensible signals.

One light between 6:00 and 7:00 p.m., for example, meant battle fleet in harbor. One light between 8:00 and 9:00 p.m. meant aircraft carriers were in the harbor, or one light between 1:00 and 2:00 a.m. meant scouting force left one to two days ago. There were also hanging-sheet signals. Two sheets on line between noon and 1:00 p.m. meant aircraft carriers left five to six days ago. And on and on it went.

Although shirts and pants on the line just meant they were doing laundry.

Kuehn was told by his handlers to go back to the drawing board. His signals were too complicated.

On December 3, 1941, Kuehn's simplified signals were transmitted to the Japanese government via shortwave radio using the secret Japanese J-19 code. American Intelligence had already broken the J-19 code. Dorothy Edgars, the only woman working in the U.S. Navy's cryptographic section, translated part of Kuehn's radio message on December 6, and even before finishing it, she alerted her male supervisor about its contents. The supervisor told her it wasn't important, and that she should go home. She stayed and finished it anyway. But then Kuehn's translated signals just sat on the supervisor's desk. As a matter of fact, two months earlier, there had been a "bomb plot" message that gave the location of every ship at anchor too, but that didn't get to the right people either, because it wasn't deemed important enough to relay to the military commanders in Hawaii.

On December 7, 1941, the Japanese bombed Pearl Harbor for one hour and fifteen minutes, killing 2,403 Americans, destroying or damaging 19 ships and over 300 aircraft.

On December 8, the United States entered WWII. That same day, the local police found Kuehn's signals at the Japanese consulate, and they matched the translated radio message.

Kuehn and his wife and stepdaughter were taken into custody. At first, Kuehn denied everything, but by December 30, he had signed a confession. On February 21, 1942, Kuehn was found guilty by a military court and given a death sentence.

His trial was the first espionage case after the outbreak of WWII, but the facts of his case and his sentence were kept confidential because Military Intelligence didn't want them released. When they finally agreed to share Kuehn's story with the press, a year and a half later, they were adamant that there be "no reference to the fact that the Americans had cracked the Japanese code." They worried that if people knew they had read the messages before the attack on Pearl Harbor, they'd be blamed for not stopping it. This information was intentionally withheld from the American public for decades, until a time when it would be easier to accept.

Otto Kuehn may have been spineless, but he did have a butt and he wanted to save it. In the blink of an eye, Otto Kuehn switched sides again; he told the U.S. government everything he knew about his Japanese and German spy buddies. Because of that cooperation, Bernard Otto Kuehn's sentence was reduced to fifty years of hard

labor. After WWII ended, he was deported back to Germany. He had spent only four years in jail.

He was an evil snake who betrayed his friends and coworkers

more than once, and he betrayed his homeland. He was an informant turned spy turned traitor turned double traitor.

Kuehn let himself be led down the wrong path. When you don't have a moral compass for what's right and wrong, it can have deadly consequences. Maybe there's a reason why everyone is always asking you what you want to be when you grow up. The real question is *who* do you want to be? Otto Kuehn never figured out who he was, so life's circumstances figured it out for him.

Bernard Otto Kuehn's story has rarely been told. His FBI files only became declassified in 1986—forty-four years after Pearl Harbor.

EVIL

BERNARD OTTO KUEHN
FACTS AND STATS

76 DAYS after the bombing of Pearl Harbor, Kuehn was found guilty and sentenced to death by a firing squad. The War Department worried that if the original sentence was carried out, Americans living in Germany and Japan might be retaliated against. Kuehn spent only four years in jail before being deported.

- **2,403 PEOPLE** were killed at Pearl Harbor.
- **1,178 PEOPLE** were injured.
- **328 U.S. AIRCRAFT** were damaged or destroyed.
- **16 U.S. SHIPS** were damaged.
- **3 U.S. SHIPS** were destroyed.
- **8 FLEET MOVEMENTS** were communicated by Kuehn to the Japanese.

THIS IS THE SIMPLIFIED VERSION OF KUEHN'S SIGNALS!

   #1 — battle fleet prepared to leave
   #2 — scouting force prepared to leave
   #3 — battle fleet left 1 to 3 days ago
   #4 — scouting fleet left 1 to 3 days ago
   #5 — aircraft carriers left 1 to 3 days ago
   #6 — battle fleet left 4 to 6 days ago
   #7 — scouting force left 4 to 6 days ago
   #8 — aircraft carriers left 4 to 6 days ago

Kuehn Had Many Ways to Signal
the Japanese About These 8 Options

Want ads
Chinese rug for
sale #3 and #6

Beauty parlor
operator #4 and #7

Lights from a window or a car
One light between 7 and 8 p.m. —#1
One light between 8 and 9 p.m. —#2
One light between 9 and 10 p.m. —#3
One light between 10 and 11 p.m. —#4
Two lights between 7 and 8 p.m. —#5
Two lights between 8 and 9 p.m. —#6
Two lights between 9 and 10 p.m. —#7
Two lights between 10 and 11 p.m. —#8

Shortwave radio
Signals could be relayed
by shortwave radio.

Sheets on a clothesline
One sheet between 8 and 9 a.m. —#1
One sheet between 9 and 10 a.m. —#2
One sheet between 10 and 11 a.m. —#3
One sheet between 11 and noon —#4
Two sheets between 8 and 9 a.m. —#5
Two sheets between 9 and 10 a.m. —#6
Two sheets between 10 and 11 a.m. —#7
Two sheets between 11 and noon —#8

Star boat (keelboat)
Signals could also be
seen on a nearby boat.
At certain times there would
be a star and a number on the sail.

Bonfires
A fire at a prescribed location
between certain hours would
correspond to the numbers above.

3 WAR WARNINGS were ignored.

January 7, 1941

U.S. Ambassador to Japan Joseph Grew communicated to authorities in Washington that the Japanese were planning to attack Pearl Harbor. No one believed the ambassador.

November 27, 1941

Admiral Husband E. Kimmel and General Walter C. Short received a "war warning" from Washington that described an imminent attack by the Japanese on the United States in the Pacific.

December 3, 1941

Otto Kuehn's secret signals were delivered to the Japanese. The message had been decoded and deemed unimportant.

 Otto Kuehn's wife was in jail with him at first but not convicted of any crime. His family was interned in Hawaii until the end of the war.

WORLD WAR II SLANG

- **Behavior Report:** a letter home to a girl
- **Devil's Piano:** a machine gun
- **Dodo:** an air force soldier who cannot fly yet
- **Eggs:** bombs
- **Fish:** torpedoes
- **Juice Jerker:** electrician
- **Kite:** airplane
- **Legs:** landing gear
- **Penguin:** an air force soldier who does not fly
- **Roll Up Your Flaps:** Stop talking
- **Taxi Up:** Come here

ANNA ANDERSON

DUCHESS DOPPELGÄNGER

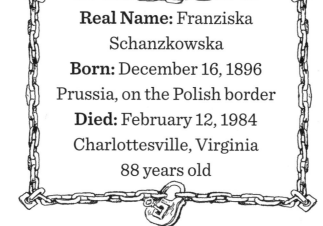

Real Name: Franziska Schanzkowska
Born: December 16, 1896
Prussia, on the Polish border
Died: February 12, 1984
Charlottesville, Virginia
88 years old

Once upon a time, there was a young woman who didn't want to be who she really was, so she pretended to be a duchess in a little plot she hatched while she was an inmate at an insane asylum. Not just any duchess either, but *the* Duchess Anastasia Romanov of Russia, who at seventeen was reportedly shot at point-blank range by the Russian revolutionaries along with the rest of her family: the tsar, the tsarina, three sisters, and a brother. The execution was so monstrous, people could barely believe it. So they didn't. This play-acting young woman was five years older than Anastasia and didn't even speak Russian. She wouldn't let anyone see her face, and couldn't remember a thing about anything, but there was no glass slipper to prove her wrong, so this sort of close look-alike turned her life into the Princess Diaries.

Her real name was Franziska Schanzkowska, and she was from Poland. Franziska believed she was better than her family of farmers, and while they gathered hay, she sat around daydreaming about being an actress. At eighteen, she moved to Berlin, Germany, to be one, but things didn't go well. While waiting to be discovered, the self-centered schemer took various jobs, including waitressing and working at a brewery. Daydreaming while working at a weapons factory, she dropped a grenade and killed the man next to her. Franziska was peppered with shrapnel. Her wounds healed, but during the following years, she was in and out of hospitals for overdosing on pills. In a grand finale she jumped off a bridge into a canal. After being fished out of the water, she was taken to a hospital.

Whether she was trying to kill herself or not, she wouldn't admit that she was Franziska Schanzkowska ever again. So she just stopped talking. The doctors at the hospital called her "Miss Unknown," and after six weeks of not speaking, she was taken to an insane asylum. Franziska didn't mind at all because she discovered the real joy of staying in bed all day and being served. Clara, a fellow patient, read a newspaper article about the murdered Russian royals with the caption "Is One of the Daughters Alive?" This was an actual possibility because the murders had been confirmed three years before, but none of their dead bodies had been found. Clara told Miss Unknown, "I know who you are. You are Grand Duchess Tatiana."

Franziska said nothing.

Clara enticed an ex-guard of the Russian royal family to meet Franziska and to confirm her hunch. The guard agreed it was Tatiana because he thought she had a dismissive and regal air. He promised to be at her service.

Franziska silently played along.

Could it be true? A daughter had survived the brutal murder! It was a story everyone wanted to believe, including Zinaida Tolstoy, the wife of Russia's best storyteller; she thought Franziska had the eyes of the tsar. A who's who of Russian society started showing up at the mental hospital. Scared she'd get caught faking it, Franziska dove under the covers when anyone came. She was a big hit until an ex-lady-in-waiting wrestled Franziska out from under the covers and declared, "She's too short for Tatiana."

Franziska realized the game was up. It was Clara's idea. Franziska didn't want to be blamed, so she finally spoke, "I never said I was Tatiana."

What? Clara had already planned a publicity tour! The two schemers looked at each other; they both knew this duchess business was so much more fun than their real lives. Okay, she couldn't be Tatiana. But what about one of these other sisters on this list? Franziska crossed out every name but Anastasia's.

Game back on.

Anastasia was the youngest daughter of the four duchesses. This was an even better fairy tale–fantasy. Everyone started calling Franziska Anna, short for Anastasia. The hoax was so good, and people wanted to believe it so much, help came rushing in. It was bye-bye, insane asylum, and hello, easy living at a baron's estate. But Anna didn't like all the parties with Russian aristocrats. This role was harder than she thought. She needed more acting lessons. She couldn't even speak Russian and she wasn't recognizing people she should have known.

Thinking she had blown it, Anna snuck away. A few days later she turned up at the Berlin zoo.

Feeling sorry for her, a police inspector let Anna stay at his home. It was going to take an award-winning performance to keep the inspector from sending her to a Gulag labor camp. Anna's duchess impersonation included staying in bed all day and complaining about the tea, the food, and

the lousy flower arrangements. The inspector kicked her out after Anastasia's aunt, Princess Irene, popped in unannounced and Anna didn't know her, but she should have. Irene said, "She could not be one of my nieces."

Luckily, Anna's fairy godmother showed up, Harriet von Rathlef-Kleilmann. Anna moved in with her. She was a fairy-tale writer and she wrote a book about how the name Anastasia meant "the resurrection" and how Anna had two life lines in both palms of her hands. And Anna's scars were just like ones Anastasia had here and there on her body. Anna didn't mention the grenade explosion.

Another supporter was the real Anastasia's childhood friend Gleb Botkin. He got busy writing books about Anna being the real Anastasia.

Many writers were anxious to rewrite this piece of gruesome history with a happy ending. There were songs, movies, plays, candy, and cigarettes named after her. The Anastasia Cult liked Anna's dismissive I'm-too-good-to-talk-to-you attitude. When asked about how she'd escaped the execution, she'd run off as if her memories were too painful. And of course, why would she ever speak Russian again after what happened to her? They didn't care that she looked old, didn't eat gravy because it reminded her of blood, and spent days in her room talking to her parrots in Polish, or that the Schanzkowska family occasionally showed up telling everyone Anna's real name is Franziska Schanzkowska. And no one saw her whole face because she covered her toothless mouth with a tissue.

The Imperial dentist said there was no way she was Anastasia. "Would I have left the teeth of one of the grand duchesses in this condition?" It's not her.

A stream of other specialists confirmed the bony bumps on their feet were the same, their handwriting was identical, and their ears matched in seventeen anatomical ways. Finally, Anna was psychoanalyzed. The psychiatrist said despite the "narrow range of her intellect" she comes from an "extremely decadent family." And her "curious amnesia" was a deliberate escape.

This was good news to Anna. She could do "curious amnesia" all day.

The people related to the actual Anastasia knew this faker was just a crackpot. When Anna hired a lawyer to get the tsar's inheri-

tance money, and she didn't even spell Anastasia correctly, eleven real Romanovs signed a statement declaring she was NOT Anastasia.

But Anna had gotten enough bravos for her performances that no one scared her anymore. She ranted to anyone who would listen, "I am the daughter of your emperor." She'd throw things out windows, attack people with sticks, and run around on the roof naked. In one temper tantrum, she stepped on her parrot and killed it. Then she wouldn't let anyone take away the dead body.

The rich people putting Anna up called the local insane asylum. But doctors declared Anna sane! For her to impersonate another would require intelligence, self-control, and discipline, "all qualities Frau Tschaikovsky in no way possesses." Tschaikovsky was another made-up last name Anna used.

A distant Romanov relative and séance enthusiast, Prince Frederick, bought Anna a fourteen-by-eighteen-foot empty army barrack in the Black Forest (known for trees and cuckoo clocks). It wasn't a castle. She was definitely taking a step down, but finally she had her own place and she could slam the door shut and be herself. She got four dogs and forty cats. Her barrack was on the Black Forest Bus Tour of Stars' Homes, so she slathered tree trunks with lard so intruders couldn't climb them to spy on her. After ten years the place was encrusted with cat poop, empty cans of food, tchotchkes, and junk. It was such a disaster the place had to be demolished.

Without any place to go, the real Anastasia's old friend Gleb Botkin persuaded the colorful millionaire-genealogist-dabbler Jack Manahan of Charlottesville, Virginia, to take care of Anna.

Anna departed the Black Forest, said goodbye to no one, and went to America to meet Jack.

Jack was as unstable as Anna. He was also twenty years younger, but he married her anyway. They made a good match. Anna liked to hide, and Jack liked to talk. When journalists showed up to meet her, he would read from books about her while she pretend-cried in the corner.

They were both hoarders of rotting bric-a-brac and were animal lovers. To protect themselves from visitors they covered the porch with banana peels. Jack bought her a tree stump to remind her of the Black Forest, which they kept in the living room.

They both believed in reincarnation and that their six Labrador puppies were the Imperial Family come back to life. They hadn't vacuumed in six years and there were cockroaches everywhere. Neighbors complained of the smell. The postman refused to go near the house, so there were piles of unopened mail in the street. They never closed their doors and never turned the heat on.

Eventually, Anna needed an intestinal operation. She also had arthritis in her feet, which made walking painful, so she mostly just lived in her car, like it was some kind of mobile home.

A couple of years later she was moved to a nursing home. Anna died of a stroke on February 12, 1984. Sixty-four years of pretending was over.

Nine years after her death, DNA tests were done with a lock of her hair and tissue samples the doctor had saved from her intestinal operation.

Franziska Schanzkowska was no Romanov.

Funny thing, she was a one hundred percent match with the Schanzkowska family, like they had been saying all along.

So don't forget, no matter how many movies and books there are about Duchess Anastasia surviving, or how many other imposters claimed to be her, it's all make-believe. Anastasia died with the rest of her family.

The senseless murder of the tsar's children had been true, and technology ended the fairy-tale version that the world found so easy to swallow. Franziska's somewhat close doppelgänger looks, and her delusions offering an iota of hope, made the perfect bandage for the times—until it was ripped off.

ANNA ANDERSON/FRANZISKA SCHANZKOWSKA FACTS AND STATS

THE REAL ROMANOVS:

On July 17, 1918, the Tsar Nicholas II; his wife, Alexandra; and their five children, Olga, Tatiana, Maria, Anastasia, and Alexei, were murdered. All their remains, except those of Anastasia and her brother, Alexei, were found in 1991. It wasn't until 2007 that Anastasia's and Alexei's remains were found and identified. Anastasia is buried in a crypt in St. Petersburg with her family.

5 FACTS to know about DNA:

- DNA is short for deoxyribonucleic acid.
- DNA found in the nucleus of a cell is called nuclear DNA.
- Nuclear DNA contains genetic information from both parents.
- Every living cell has many DNA molecules.
- No two people have the exact same DNA.

DNA AND SOLVING CRIMES:

DNA evidence left behind at a crime scene—like blood, saliva, hair, teeth, and fingernails—can help identify who was involved. DNA can be found on things like cigarettes, cups, clothes, and weapons.

1st DNA used in a legal case was to prove identity, not to solve a crime.

In 1985, Christiana Sarbah's teenage son had arrived in England from Ghana without his papers. England's Home Office accepted DNA evidence that proved their mother-son relationship, and the boy was allowed to stay with his mother.

1st CRIMINAL CASE that used DNA evidence to solve a crime was in Leicestershire, England, in 1987. DNA evidence proved the innocence of one suspect and convicted the true murderer.

1st PERSON convicted on DNA evidence was Tommy Lee Andrews.

73 PERCENT OF THE INNOCENCE PROJECT'S 239 overturned convictions had been originally based on eyewitness testimony. The Innocence Project, which was established in the 1990s, uses DNA testing to clear wrongfully convicted individuals.

17 ANATOMICAL POINTS and tissue formations on Anna's ears matched Anastasia's. Only twelve points were normally needed to confirm identity. Experts concluded that Anna's ears matched Anastasia's. **WRONG**

14 HOURS a day for one year Professor Otto Reche analyzed photos of Anna Anderson and Anastasia. He concluded they were the same person based on these four comparisons:

• Width of their cheekbones
• Relationship of the lower jaw to the cheekbones
• Position and size of the eye sockets
• Width of the forehead

Dr. Reche said, "Such coincidence between two human faces is not possible except when they are the same person, or identical twins." **WRONG**

3 HANDWRITING EXPERTS (graphologists) analyzed Anna Anderson's handwriting. They all agreed Anna Anderson was most likely Grand Duchess Anastasia. **WRONG**

137 POINTS on Anna's and Anastasia's handwriting samples matched, according to graphologist Minna Becker. She concluded that, "with a probability bordering on certainty," Anna Anderson was Anastasia. **WRONG**

 GRAPHOLOGIST Minna Becker authenticated the diaries of Anne Frank.

Synonyms for *Doppelgänger*

(derived from German, meaning "ghostly double")

- Copy
- Duplicate
- Identical
- Lookalike

- Match
- One and the Same
- Take After
- Twin

Synonyms for *Impostor*

- Bluffer
- Cheat
- Con Man
- Deceiver
- Deluder

- Fake
- Falsifier
- Fraud
- Trickster
- Usurper

AL CAPONE

THE WORLD ACCORDING TO AL CAPONE

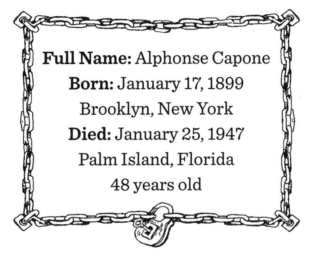

Full Name: Alphonse Capone
Born: January 17, 1899
Brooklyn, New York
Died: January 25, 1947
Palm Island, Florida
48 years old

Al Capone was 100 percent gangster with a mastermind for running illegal businesses that made him rich. "Public service is my motto," he said. His definition of *public service* included drive-by shootings, baseball-bat beatings, and election fraud. He was into illegal drinking, gambling, and prostitution, of which he said, "Most guys hurt people. I don't hurt nobody. Only them that get in my way." Normally, gangsters who think like that don't advertise it with grammatically incorrect statements. Rules didn't apply to Capone, grammar or otherwise. He wasn't book smart, but his kind of street smarts kept him rolling in the dough. He had more custom-tailored suits in his wardrobe than words in his vocabulary because he had a lot of illegal money and he liked spending it. He was a big show-off too. The word *shopaholic* hadn't been invented yet, but he definitely was one, and that behavior would be his downfall.

Al Capone was born in Brooklyn, New York, in 1899. His dad was a barber and his mom was raising nine kids. As the fourth kid and fourth boy in his big Italian family, Al was the classic middle child—slipping through the cracks unnoticed. At fourteen he was still in grammar school, repeating sixth grade, until Al punched his teacher and promoted himself to the school of crime on the streets of Brooklyn. Classes were replaced with pool halls and gangs, and his new mentors were all the wrong people. Al interned at gambling halls and nightclubs. By the time he was nineteen, he was a murderer, and he earned the catchy nickname Scarface after he was knifed three times in the cheek.

Mary Coughlin liked Al's scars enough and became his bride-to-be. Their son was inconveniently born three weeks before they tied the knot, which would qualify it as a shotgun wedding (how fitting), but conveniently timed to keep Capone from serving in the army during World War I (not to mention he had registered late for the draft).

While two million other Americans went off to battle, all Al had to do was obey the wartime ban on alcohol and then the Eighteenth Amendment to the U.S. Constitution, known as Prohibition, which made selling or buying alcohol illegal. Just ordering a cocktail became a federal offense, which was practically impossible to enforce, so Al made a killing illegally selling alcohol. And then after the war, Prohibition met its match in the Roaring Twenties, when Americans were in a carefree mood that included a lot of drinking and some new vocabulary for Al to learn. Alcohol was renamed *moonshine,* because it often had to be made in the middle of the night to keep it on the down low. *Bootleggers* transported the moonshine (hidden in their boots). And *speakeasies* were illegal bars where drinkers could sneak moonshine.

Al Capone became Mr. Moonshiner and Bootlegger in Chief. By the time he was twenty-five, he owned thousands of illegal businesses—speakeasies, breweries, gambling dens, brothels, dog races, and horse-betting parlors—in Chicago, Illinois. His personal seven-hundred-man army did shady things on his orders, like assassinate the competition with bombs or machine guns, hijack other bootleggers' trucks, and steal ballot boxes to help get the right people elected who wouldn't arrest him. His yearly income from all his businesses was about one hundred million dollars, which today is about one billion dollars. Even though everything he did was against the law, Capone actually bought business cards and fancy suits like he was a regular businessman.

Except most businessmen don't have office doors made of steel, or bodyguards with bulletproof vests out front, or secret tunnels connected to the garage, leading to a steel-plated Cadillac sedan with bulletproof windows.

Capone also had to pay for a different kind of "protection." Police, Prohibition agents, and politicians were paid low wages, so when Al paid them extra money *not* to arrest him, they were happy to oblige. Not to mention if they didn't take it, he'd just eliminate them from the planet. The results were amazing. A person could be standing there one minute and gone the next. If witnesses to his crimes didn't seal their lips, they were "taken for a ride," which meant they were dead.

Capone owned everyone in town because, like he said, "You can get a lot farther with a smile and a gun than you can get with just a smile."

Unlike normal gun-toting mobsters who wanted to be hard to find, Capone had a constant urge to be seen in his loud checkerboard suits. He'd throw silver dollars out his car window or he'd stop and shake hands with people along the side of the road. Practically every day he'd parade up and down the streets in front of city hall to show everybody who was really in charge. He invited gossip columnists into his home for "off the record" chats and a chance to take his photo. To guarantee his own good press, a reporter who was going to print a negative article about Capone was mysteriously kidnapped, handcuffed, blindfolded, and dropped in the woods. Capone was Mr. Glamorous Gangster, and Hollywood made movies about guys like Capone—a gangster with a heart of gold.

People were bamboozled by Capone's showy facade for a while, until Chicago became the murder capital of the United States. In 1928, there were 367 gangland-style murders. At first it was just gangsters whacking each other, but then Capone killed the city prosecutor, the police chief, and a journalist. Not to mention the machine-gun bloodbath when seven people were killed on St. Valentine's Day. This scared everybody straight.

Capone wasn't looking so dazzling anymore, especially after the Chicago Crime Commission gave Capone top billing as Public Enemy Number 1. But he wasn't just Chicago's problem; he was the nation's problem.

Stopping him wasn't going to be easy. Prohibition agents like Eliot Ness were wiretapping phones and smashing up Capone's breweries with battering rams. The latest cutting-edge ballistic technology was being used to analyze crime-scene bullets and match them to the weapons of Al Capone's hit men.  But behind the scenes, the real case against Capone was being figured out by bespectacled number crunchers with pencils and paper.

Practically everybody else in the United States except Al Capone was number crunching too. The roaring fun parts of the 1920s were over. By 1929 it was the Great Depression. Al was spending millions while everyone else was in line for bread and soup—and he hardly noticed.

He also didn't care that the U.S. Supreme Court ruled that crooks had to pay taxes on their illegal income. "The income tax law is a lot of bunk," he said.

Except that the "bunk" was hitting the fan.

In 1931, thirty-two-year-old Al Capone was charged with income tax evasion. *The United States v. Alphonse Capone* was the result of a four-year effort of snooping into Al Capone's records and getting a few of his bookkeepers to risk their lives by ratting on him. Since there was no such thing as the Witness Protection Program at the time, one witness snuck off to South America and another went to Oregon to guarantee they'd still be breathing when they were called to testify at the trial.

On October 7, 1931, looking like a big blow-up pool toy stuffed into a blue suit and with a blubbery smile plastered on his face, Al Capone was greeted at the courthouse by forty policemen. Capone wasn't worried; he had already bribed the jurors with $1,000 bills (those existed back then).

Too bad Capone's lawyers relied less on figuring out his case than jury tampering, because the judge immediately replaced the jury. To cut out the possibility of Capone bribing the new jury, the judge arranged a confined jury sleepover. Behaving according to the Court's rules was not part of Al's plan. Even though it was illegal to bring a weapon, he brought his gun-toting bodyguard into the courthouse with him, until the judge threw the body-guard out. There was another big surprise; the prosecutors were going to prove Capone owed income taxes by showing how much money he spent. They had followed the money backward. His name wasn't on any bank deposit slips, but he was a proud customer at practically every

store in town. The prosecutors' smoking gun was Capone's shopping habits. If he had all that money to spend, he must have made some money, but Capone had never, ever filed income tax returns.

Capone started smiling less.

Fifty witnesses testified about Capone's shopping sprees: build-ers, butchers, hotel clerks, interior decorators, and store managers. He bought rugs, cars, sterling silver, showy doodads, and a total of thirty diamond-studded belt buckles. By the dozen, he bought shirts, ties, collars, and handkerchiefs. His passion for Italian-made, full-body silk underwear, the kind with a button flap in the back, was revealed to the jury and then printed in the newspaper.

His once adoring fans were now cracking jokes about his silk-undies shopping sprees. And it took the jury only about nine hours to decide Al Capone was guilty of income tax evasion.

But reality still wasn't sinking in; Capone had a few days off before his sentencing, and his first thought showed he'd learned nothing. He told a loyal partner in crime, "I need some new clothes before I go."

He didn't need to bother; the judge sentenced Capone to eleven years of wearing prison stripes. As the jail wardens led Al Capone to his cell, he called out to the cameramen, "Please don't take my picture."

That was a first.

Capone tried running his business out of his Cook County Jail cell, but it didn't last long.

The only smarts he had were street smarts. "I could bear it all if it weren't for the hurt it brings to my mother and my family." He should have thought of that sooner.

Capone had run a secret underworld of assassins, gunmen, and thugs who did whatever he told them. His expensive lifestyle and fake smile fooled everybody for a while, until the law and war of words and numbers caught up with him.

Al Capone served time in Cook County Jail, U.S. Penitentiary, in Atlanta, and at the legendary maximum-security prison called Alcatraz. He served only seven years and six months of his eleven-year sentence. He was released on November 16, 1939, because of bad health. He suffered from an advanced case of syphilis. It deteriorated his brain, which caused mood swings, delusions of grandeur, and thinking and speech problems.

He lived the last seven years of his life with the mentality of a twelve-year-old kid. Al Capone was back in sixth grade at forty years old, and he was never going to graduate.

AL CAPONE FACTS AND STATS

WISDOM OF AL CAPONE:

"I don't want to die. Especially I don't want to die in the street, punctured with machine-gun bullets."

"You can all go thirsty."

"I've never been convicted of a crime nor have I ever directed anyone else to commit a crime."

"You'd think I was Jesse James and the Youngers, all in one."

10 **PUBLIC ENEMIES** were on the first list created in 1930 by Frank J. Loesch, the head of the Chicago Crime Commission. Al Capone was Public Enemy Number 1, his brother Ralph was number 2. Numbers 3, 4, and 5 were men in Capone's mob.

#1. Alphonse Capone

#2. Ralph Capone

#3. Frank Rio

#4. Jack McGurn

#5. Jack Guzick

FBI director J. Edgar Hoover copied the Public Enemies List. He called it FBI's "Ten Most Wanted."

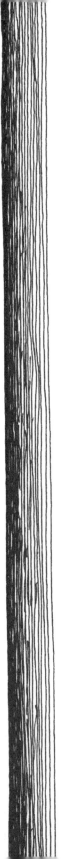

6 GANGSTERS' NICKNAMES:

Scarface: Al Capone
Bugs: George Moran
Dingbat: John Oberta
Bingo: John Alberto
Schemer: Vincent Drucci
Loud Mouth: Hymie Levin

8,600 WITNESSES have been protected and relocated under the U.S. Marshals Service's **Witness Protection Program** since its inception in 1970. Not one witness or any of their 9,900 family members have been harmed.

24-HOUR PROTECTION is provided for witnesses worried about retaliation by criminals they testify against. They also receive new identities, a new place to live, health care, job training, and employment assistance.
In Al Capone's time, witnesses were not protected.

3 THINGS forensic ballistics experts look for when examining firearms evidence:

- Size of the bullet: caliber of the weapon
- Rifling marks: distinct pattern left on the bullet after it goes through the barrel

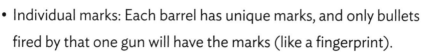

- Individual marks: Each barrel has unique marks, and only bullets fired by that one gun will have the marks (like a fingerprint).

If a bullet has been used in a crime, it is entered into a law enforcement database so it can be connected to other crimes.

1925 **WAS THE YEAR** Calvin Hooker Goddard, Charles Waite, and Philip Gravelle founded the **Bureau of Forensic Ballistics** in NYC. It wasn't until the St. Valentine's Day Massacre four years later that forensic ballistics received wide attention and respect when the ballistics reports from that crime scene were printed in the newspapers.

ST. VALENTINE'S DAY MASSACRE BY THE NUMBERS:

- 2 Tommy guns present
- 4 killers
- 2 bad guys dressed as policemen
- 7 men lined up against a wall
- 90 bullets fired
- 6 men DOA (dead on arrival)
- 1 man left alive to spill the beans
- 0 names given

BOOTLEGGER'S DICTIONARY

- **Bootleg:** illegally transported liquor; comes from jamming a bottle inside a boot to hide it
- **Flapper:** young, carefree woman of the 1920s and '30s who cut her hair short, listened to jazz, and drank alcohol
- **Henchman:** personal assistant willing to kill for you
- **Jazz:** music that originated in African American communities and became popular in the 1920s; often performed in speakeasies
- **Moonshine:** illegally made liquor produced in the dead of night
- **Racketeering:** Organized bullying. An illegal group collects fees and threatens to bomb, slug, and kill business owners if they don't pay up.
- **Speakeasy:** A secret, forbidden drinking bar. Customers had to keep quiet about them.
- **Tommy Gun:** nickname for the Thompson submachine gun; a gangster's favorite gun

ACKNOWLEDGMENTS

Thanks to Leah Komaiko and Angela Wiencek-Ashe for always saying yes when I need their help. With great love and appreciation I thank Victoria Beck, Christine Bernardi, Edith Cohn, Tracy Holczer, Leslie Margolis, Elizabeth Passarelli, and Anne Reinhard.

I'd like to thank reading teacher Lindsey Hughes and her students at Florida's Baker County High School for giving me detailed notes on an early draft of "Al Capone." Best of all, they shared some of their beautiful poems with me. And thanks to Jennifer Smith and her children's literature students at Austin College for their notes and teacher-guide recommendations on "Blackbeard."

Of course, I want to thank Edward Necarsulmer IV and Emily Easton.

BIBLIOGRAPHY

Sources for direct quotations and further reading can be found at:
georgiabragg.com/bookspage/caught

PRINT SOURCES

JOAN OF ARC

DeVries, Kelly. *Joan of Arc: A Military Leader.* Phoenix Mill: Sutton Publishing Limited, 1999.

Fabre, Lucien. *Joan of Arc,* trans. Gerard Hopkins. New York: McGraw-Hill Book Company Inc., 1954.

Harrison, Kathryn. *Joan of Arc: A Life Transfigured.* New York: Doubleday, 2014.

Pernoud, Régine. *The Retrial of Joan of Arc: The Evidence at the Trial for Her Rehabilitation 1450–1456,* trans. J. M. Cohen. New York: Harcourt, Brace and Company, Inc., 1955.

Pernoud, Régine, and Marie-Véronique Clin. *Joan of Arc: Her Story,* trans. Jeremy DuQuesnay Adams. New York: St. Martin's Press, 1998.

Spoto, Donald. *Joan: The Mysterious Life of the Heretic Who Became a Saint.* New York: HarperSanFrancisco, 2007.

Taylor, Larissa Juliet. *The Virgin Warrior: The Life and Death of Joan of Arc.* New Haven: Yale University Press, 2009.

SIR WALTER RALEIGH

Beer, Anna. *My Just Desire: The Life of Bess Raleigh, Wife to Sir Walter.* New York: Ballantine Books, 2003.

Doran, Susan. *Elizabeth I and Her Circle.* Oxford: Oxford University Press, 2015.

Doran, Susan. *Queen Elizabeth I.* New York: New York University Press, 2003.

Gristwood, Sarah. *Elizabeth and Leicester: Power, Passion, Politics.* New York: Viking, 2007.

Kirsch, Jonathan. *The Grand Inquisitor's Manual: A History of Terror in the Name of God.* New York: HarperOne, 2008.

Ross, Josephine. *Suitors to the Queen: The Men in the Life of Elizabeth I of England.* New York: Coward, McCann & Geoghegan, 1975.

Weir, Alison. *The Life of Elizabeth I.* New York: Ballantine Books, 2008.

Williams, Neville. *All the Queen's Men: Elizabeth and Her Courtiers.* New York: Macmillan Company, 1972.

CARAVAGGIO

Graham-Dixon, Andrew. *Caravaggio: A Life Sacred and Profane.* New York: W. W. Norton & Company, 2010.

Langdon, Helen. *Caravaggio: A Life.* New York: Farrar, Straus and Giroux, 1998.

Prose, Francine. *Caravaggio: Painter of Miracles.* New York: Harper Perennial, 2005.

BLACKBEARD

Burgess, Douglas R., Jr. *The Pirates' Pact: The Secret Alliances Between History's Most Notorious Buccaneers and Colonial America.* New York: McGraw Hill, 2009.

Cordingly, David. *Under the Black Flag: The Romance and the Reality of Life Among the Pirates.* New York: Random House Trade Paperbacks, 2006.

George, Rose. *Ninety Percent of Everything: Inside Shipping, the Invisible Industry That Puts Clothes on Your Back, Gas in Your Car, and Food on Your Plate.* New York: Metropolitan Books, 2013.

Langewiesche, William. *The Outlaw Sea: A World of Freedom, Chaos, and Crime.* New York: North Point Press, 2004.

Latimer, Jon. *Buccaneers of the Caribbean: How Piracy Forged an Empire.* Cambridge: Harvard University Press, 2009.

Paine, Lincoln P. *Ships of the World: An Historical Encyclopedia.* Boston: Houghton Mifflin Company, 1997.

Rediker, Marcus. *Between the Devil and the Deep Blue Sea: Merchant Seamen, Pirates, and the Anglo-American Maritime World, 1700–1750.* 15th ed. Cambridge: Cambridge University Press, 2010.

Rediker, Marcus. *Villains of All Nations: Atlantic Pirates in the Golden Age.* Boston: Beacon Press, 2004.

Woodard, Colin. *The Republic of Pirates: Being the True and Surprising Story of the Caribbean Pirates and the Man Who Brought Them Down.* Orlando: Harcourt Inc., 2007.

JOHN WILKES BOOTH

Alford, Terry. *Fortune's Fool: The Life of John Wilkes Booth.* Oxford: Oxford University Press, 2015.

Bogar, Thomas A. *Backstage at the Lincoln Assassination: The Untold Story of the Actors and Stagehands at Ford's Theatre.* Washington: Regnery History, 2013.

Hunt, Mitchell M. *The Lincoln Assassination Documents.* Norman: MMH Publishing, 2014.

Swanson, James L. *Manhunt: The Twelve-Day Chase for Lincoln's Killer.* New York: Harper Perennial, 2006.

JESSE JAMES

Bruns, Roger A. *The Bandit Kings: From Jesse James to Pretty Boy Floyd.* New York: Crown Publishers, Inc., 1995.

Enss, Chris. *Principles of Posse Management: Lessons from the Wild West.* Lanham, MD: Rowman & Littlefield Publishing Group, Inc., 2018.

Gardner, Mark Lee. *Shot All to Hell: Jesse James, the Northfield Raid, and the Wild West's Greatest Escape.* New York: William Morrow, 2013.

Muehlberger, James P. *The Lost Cause: The Trials of Frank and Jesse James.* Yardley: Westholme, 2013.

Settle, William A., Jr. *Jesse James Was His Name: Or, Fact and Fiction Concerning the Careers of the Notorious James Brothers of Missouri.* Columbia: University of Missouri Press, 1966.

Stiles, T. J. *Jesse James: Last Rebel of the Civil War.* New York: Alfred A. Knopf, 2002.

Yeatman, Ted P. *Frank and Jesse James: The Story Behind the Legend.* Nashville: Cumberland House, 2000.

BILLY THE KID

Cline, Donald. *Alias Billy the Kid: The Man Behind the Legend.* Santa Fe: Sunstone Press, 1986.

Coe, George W., and Nan Hillary Harrison. *Frontier Fighter: The Autobiography of George W. Coe, Who Fought and Rode with Billy the Kid.* Albuquerque: University of New Mexico Press, 1934.

Gardner, Mark Lee. *To Hell on a Fast Horse: The Untold Story of Billy the Kid and Pat Garrett.* New York: Harper, 2010.

Garrett, Pat F. *The Authentic Life of Billy the Kid.* New York: Skyhorse Publishing, 2011.

Jameson, W. C. *Billy the Kid: Beyond the Grave.* Lanham: Taylor Trade Publishing, 2008.

Siringo, Chas. A. *History of "Billy the Kid."* Lago Vista: Grindl Press, 2013.

Utley, Robert M. *Billy the Kid: A Short and Violent Life.* Lincoln: University of Nebraska Press, 1989.

Walker, Dale L. *Legends and Lies: Great Mysteries of the American West.* New York: Tom Doherty Associates, 1997.

Wallis, Michael. *Billy the Kid: The Endless Ride.* New York: W. W. Norton & Company, 2007.

MATA HARI

Ostrovsky, Erika. *Eye of Dawn: The Rise and Fall of Mata Hari.* New York: MacMillan Publishing Co., Inc., 1978.
Shipman, Pat. *Femme Fatale: Love, Lies, and the Unknown Life of Mata Hari.* 2007. New York: Harper Perennial, 2008.
Waagenaar, Sam. *The Murder of Mata Hari.* London: Arthur Barker Limited, 1964.
Wheelwright, Julie. *The Fatal Lover: Mata Hari and the Myth of Women in Espionage.* London: Collins & Brown, 1992.

TYPHOID MARY

Bourdain, Anthony. *Typhoid Mary: An Urban Historical.* New York: Bloomsbury, 2001.
Fenster, Julie M. *Mavericks, Miracles, and Medicine: The Pioneers Who Risked Their Lives to Bring Medicine into the Modern Age.* New York: Carroll and Graf Publishers, 2003.
Leavitt, Judith Walzer. *Typhoid Mary: Captive to the Public's Health.* Boston: Beacon Press, 1996.

RASPUTIN

Fuhrmann, Joseph T. *Rasputin: The Untold Story.* Hoboken: John Wiley & Sons, Inc., 2013.
Radzinsky, Edvard. *The Rasputin File,* trans. Judson Rosengrant. New York: Anchor Books, 2000.
Rappaport, Helen. *The Last Days of the Romanovs: Tragedy at Ekaterinburg.* New York: St. Martin's Press, 2008.

VINCENZO PERUGGIA

Beavan, Colin. *Fingerprints: The Origins of Crime Detection and the Murder Case That Launched Forensic Science.* New York: Hyperion, 2001.
Cole, Simon A. *Suspect Identities: A History of Fingerprinting and Criminal Identification.* Cambridge: Harvard University Press, 2001.
McLeave, Hugh. *Rogues in the Gallery: The Modern Plague of Art Thefts.* Boston: David R. Godine, 1981.
Mohen, Jean Pierre, Michel Menu, and Bruno Mottin. Mona Lisa: *Inside the Painting.* New York: Abrams, 2006.
Pallanti, Guiseppe. Mona Lisa *Revealed: The True Identity of Leonardo's Model.* Milan: Skira, 2006.
Reit, Seymour V. *The Day They Stole the* Mona Lisa. New York: Summit Books, 1981.
Scotti, R. A. *Vanished Smile: The Mysterious Theft of* Mona Lisa. New York: Vintage Books, 2009.

BERNARD OTTO KUEHN

Clarke, Thurston. *Pearl Harbor Ghosts: The Legacy of December 7, 1941.* 2nd ed. New York: Ballantine Publishing Group, 2001.

Goodman, Michael E. *The CIA and Other American Spies.* Mankato: Creative Education, 2013.

ANNA ANDERSON

Grabbe, Alexander. *The Private World of the Last Tsar: In the Photographs and Notes of General Count Alexander Grabbe,* ed. Paul Grabbe and Beatrice Grabbe. Boston: Little, Brown & Co., 1984.

King, Greg, and Penny Wilson. *The Resurrection of the Romanovs: Anastasia, Anna Anderson, and the World's Greatest Royal Mystery.* Hoboken: John Wiley & Sons, Inc., 2011.

Kurth, Peter. *Anastasia: The Riddle of Anna Anderson.* Boston: Little, Brown & Co., 1983.

Radzinsky, Edward. *The Last Tsar: The Life and Death of Nicholas II,* trans. Marian Schwartz. New York: Doubleday, 1992.

Rappaport, Helen. *The Romanov Sisters: The Lost Lives of the Daughters of Nicholas and Alexandra.* New York: St. Martin's Press, 2014.

Steinberg, Mark D., and Vladimir M. Khrustalev. *The Fall of the Romanovs: Political Dreams and Personal Struggles in a Time of Revolution.* New Haven: Yale University Press, 1995.

Trewin, J. C. *The House of Special Purpose.* New York: Stein and Day, 1975.

AL CAPONE

Balsamo, William, and John Balsamo. *Young Al Capone: The Untold Story of Scarface in New York, 1899–1925.* New York: Skyhorse Publishing, 2011.

Bergreen, Laurence. *Capone: The Man and the Era.* New York: Simon & Schuster Paperbacks, 1994.

Earp, Mike. *U.S. Marshals: Inside America's Most Storied Law Enforcement Agency.* New York: William Morrow, 2014.

Eig, Jonathan. *Get Capone: The Secret Plot That Captured America's Most Wanted Gangster.* New York: Simon & Schuster Paperbacks, 2010.

Jeffreys-Jones, Rhodri. *The FBI: A History.* New Haven: Yale University Press, 2007.

Kurland, Michael. *Irrefutable Evidence: Adventures in the History of Forensic Science.* Chicago: Ivan R. Dee, 2009.

Nickell, Joe, and John F. Fischer. *Crime Science: Methods of Forensic Detection.* Lexington: University Press of Kentucky, 1999.

Perry, Douglas. *Eliot Ness: The Rise and Fall of an American Hero.* New York: Viking, 2014.

ONLINE SOURCES

JOAN OF ARC

"Becoming a Saint." Joan of Arc, 2005. saint-joan-of-arc.com/becoming-a-saint.htm

Catholic Online. "St. Joan of Arc." Catholic Online, 2016. catholic.org/saints/saint. php?saint_id=295

Cohen, Jennie. "7 Surprising Facts About Joan of Arc." History. A&E Networks, January 28, 2013. history.com/news/history-lists/7-surprising-facts-about-joan-of-arc

"Joan of Arc Remains 'Are Fakes.'" BBC News, April 4, 2007. news.bbc.co.uk/2/ hi/6527105.stm

Markey, Dell. "Process of Beatification in the Roman Catholic Church." The Classroom, 2016. classroom.synonym.com/process-beatification-roman-catholic-church-7713. html

"Posthumous," et al. Merriam-Webster, 2017. merriam-webster.com/dictionary/

Rothman, Lily. "How Lefties First Gained Acceptance." *Time,* August 13, 2015. time. com/3978951/lefties-history/

Williamson, Allen. "Her Signature." Joan of Arc Archive, 2004. saint-joan-of-arc.com/ signature.htm

Williamson, Allen. "Signatures & Her Name." Joan of Arc Archive, 2004. archive.joan-of-arc.org/joanofarc_signatures.html

SIR WALTER RALEIGH

"1618: Sir Walter Raleigh Executed." History. A&E Networks, 2009. history.com/this-day-in-history/sir-walter-raleigh-executed

"Privateer," et al. Merriam-Webster, 2017. merriam-webster.com/dictionary/

"Sir Walter Raleigh." Westminster Abbey. UNESCO, 2017. westminster-abbey.org/our-history/people/sir-walter-raleigh

"What Killed 'Em: Queen Elizabeth I." Medical Bag. Haymarket Media, Inc., September 27, 2012. medicalbag.com/what-killed-em/queen-elizabeth-i/article/486648/

Wolfe, Brendan. "Sir Walter Raleigh (ca. 1552–1618)." Encyclopedia Virginia. Virginia Foundation for the Humanities, June 13, 2014. encyclopediavirginia.org/Raleigh_Sir_Walter_ca_1552-1618#start_entry

CARAVAGGIO

Amy. "A Quiet Holiness: Caravaggio's Madonna Di Loreto." Caravaggista, August 5, 2013. caravaggista.com/2013/08/a-quiet-holiness-caravaggios-madonna-di-loreto/

"Bacchus." Artble, 2017. artble.com/artists/caravaggio/paintings/bacchus

"Baroque Artists." Art in the Picture, 2016. artinthepicture.com/styles/Baroque/

"Baroque Sculpture (c. 1600–1700)." Encyclopedia of Sculpture. Art Encyclopedia, 2016. visual-arts-cork.com/sculpture/baroque-sculpture.htm#sculptures

"Caravaggio: The Complete Works." Caravaggio Foundation, 2016.

Daley, Jason. "Multi-Million Dollar Painting Found in Leaky French Attic." *Smithsonian,* April 13, 2016. smithsonianmag.com/smart-news/multi-million-dollar-painting-found-leaky-french-attic-180958752/

Kington, Tom. "The Mystery of Caravaggio's Death Solved at Last—Painting Killed Him." *The Guardian,* June 16, 2010. theguardian.com/artanddesign/2010/jun/16/caravaggio-italy-remains-ravenna-art

Piperno, Roberto. "Baroque Sculpture in Rome." Rome in the Footsteps of an XVIIIth Century Traveller, n.d. Last modified November 2015. romeartlover.it/Sculptures.html

Senecal, Robert. "Carlo Borromeo's Instructiones Fabricae Et Supellectilis Ecclesiasticae and Its Origins in the Rome of His Time." *Papers of the British School at Rome,* vol. 68 (2000), pp. 241–267. jstor.org/stable/40311031

Smith, Stephen H. "Michelangelo Merisi da Caravaggio: Beneath the Surface." Three Magi, pp. 1–23. Accessed September 4, 2018. threemagi.com/art/papers/Caravaggio.pdf

BLACKBEARD

"Blackbeard's Flag, Blackbeard Flag Symbols and Meaning." Blackbeard Info, Blackbeard the Pirate Facts, 2011. blackbeardsrealm.com/Blackbeard-flag.html

Croce, Pat. "Pirates! A Curriculum-Based Educational Adventure in Pirate and Florida History." St. Augustine Pirate & Treasure Museum, 2015. thepiratemuseum.com/pirate-tours/in-class-curriculum/

"Educational Resources on Blackbeard and Maritime History." Queen Anne's Revenge Project, n.d. Accessed September 4, 2018. qaronline.org/education

"Investigating Mystery Objects: Identifying Artifacts from Blackbeard's *Queen Anne's Revenge.*" Gotricounty.com, April 18, 2014. gotricounty.com/recipes/index.php?display=detail&sp=0&tid=073633f8a15949bf28b47533ebcc4ef7&id=83d935763ba5f779e67688b910f03495

Macguire, Eoghan. "Why Scouring Sea for Sunken Treasures Is Big Business." CNN, March 14, 2012. edition.cnn.com/2012/03/13/business/sunken-treasure-business/

NC DNCR staff. "Lab Conserving Treasures Recovered from Blackbeard's Queen Anne's Revenge Shipwreck Celebrates 10 Years." North Carolina Department of Natural and Cultural Resources. May 30, 2014. ncdcr.gov/blog/2014/05/30/lab-conserving-treasures-recovered-blackbeards-queen-annes-revenge-shipwreck

Nye, Eric W. "Pounds Sterling to Dollars: Historical Conversion of Currency." University of Wyoming. n.d. Accessed September 4, 2018. uwyo.edu/numimage/currency.htm

"Pirate Dictionary." The Pirate Ship, 2014. the-pirate-ship.com/piratedictionary.html

Power, Matthew. "Hostile Takeovers." Crimes & Punishments. *Lapham's Quarterly,* Spring 2009. laphamsquarterly.org/crimes-punishments/hostile-takeovers

Yetter, George Humphrey. "When Blackbeard Scourged the Seas." The Colonial Williamsburg Foundation, Autumn 1992. history.org/Foundation/journal/blackbea.cfm

JOHN WILKES BOOTH

Arkowitz, Hal and Scott O. Lilienfeld. "Why Science Tells Us Not to Rely on Eyewitness Accounts." *Scientific American*. Nature America, Inc., January 1, 2010. scientificamerican.com/article/do-the-eyes-have-it/

Ford's Theatre Staff. "Frequently Asked Questions." Ford's Theatre. National Park Service, 2016. nps.gov/foth/faqs.htm

Ford's Theatre Staff. "Lincoln's Assassination." Ford's Theatre, 2016. fords.org/lincolns-assassination/

Hall, James O. "The Booth Family Tree." Surratt House Museum, 2016. surrattmuseum.org/booth-family-tree

"Historical Events on April 14." On This Day, 2017. onthisday.com/events/april/14

"Inflation Calculator." CPI Inflation Calculator, 2016. in2013dollars.com/1865-dollars?amount=100000

Morgan, David. "Lincoln Assassination: The Other Murder Attempt." CBS News, May 10, 2015. cbsnews.com/news/lincoln-assassination-the-other-murder-attempt/

"Presidential Assassinations, Attempts, and Security Measures." Presidentsusa.net. Baaron's Hill LLC, 2016. presidentsusa.net/assassinations.html

"Sacramentals Catalog, The." Sisters of the Passion & Cross, 2015. traditionalpoorclaremonastery.org/catalog.html

Stebner, Beth. "The Grisly Last Moments of Four Lincoln Assassination Conspirators (Including the First Woman Executed by the Government)." DailyMail.com. June 20, 2012. dailymail.co.uk/news/article-2162460/Lincoln-assassination-conspirators-Grisly-moments-Civil-War-era-prisoners-convicted-conspiring-kill-president.html

Surratt Staff. "John Wilkes Booth Escape Route Tour." Surratt House Museum, 2016. surrattmuseum.org/booth-escape-tour

Weaver, Mark. "LaFayette Baker." American Civil War Story, 2016. americancivilwarstory.com/lafayette-baker.html

Wick, Robert G. "Battle for the War Department Rewards for the Capture of John Wilkes Booth." Journal of the Abraham Lincoln Association. University of Michigan Library. Vol. 32, issue 2. September 2011. quod.lib.umich.edu/j/jala/2629860.0032.203/—battle-for-the-war-department-rewards-for-the-capture?rgn=main;view=fulltext

Wikimedia Commons. "File: John Wilkes Booth Wanted Poster Colour.png." Wikimedia Commons, August 28, 2007. commons.wikimedia.org/wiki/File:John_Wilkes_Booth_wanted_poster_colour.png

JESSE JAMES

Andrews, Evan. "10 Things You May Not Know About the Pinkertons." History. A&E Networks. October 23, 2015. history.com/news/history-lists/10-things-you-may-not-know-about-the-pinkertons

Bettinger, Blaine. "Famous DNA Review, Part IV—Jesse James." The Genetic Genealogist, February 15, 2008. thegeneticgenealogist.com/2008/02/15/famous-dna-review-part-iv-jesse-james/

"Bushwhack." Merriam-Webster, 2017. merriam-webster.com/dictionary/bushwhacker

CIA. "A Look Back . . . The Black Dispatches: Intelligence During the Civil War." CIA, February 5, 2009. cia.gov/news-information/featured-story-archive/black-dispatches.html

Kopel, David. "Sheriffs and the Posse Comitatus." In The Volokh Conspiracy. *The Washington Post,* May 15, 2014. washingtonpost.com/news/volokh-conspiracy/ wp/2014/05/15/sheriffs-and-the-posse-comitatus/?noredirect=on&utm_ term=.5ccd5c32eac9

Kozikowski, Kara E. "Guerrilla Warfare: Hometown Heroes and Villains." American Battlefield Trust. History, n.d. Accessed September 4, 2018. civilwar.org/learn/articles/ guerrilla-warfare

"Life of John Scobell, The." Prezi, May 11, 2015. prezi.com/r8uw3dh3_gkz/the-life-of-john-scobell/

Nix, Elizabeth. "7 Things You May Not Know About Jesse James." History. A&E Networks, December 8, 2014. history.com/news/history-lists/7-things-you-might-not-know-about-jesse-james

Paulfrasercollectibles. "Jesse James Wanted Poster Beats Estimate by 129.9%." Just Collecting, 2014. justcollecting.com/miscellania/jesse-james-wanted-poster-beats-estimate-by-129-9

PBS Staff. "Allan Pinkerton's Detective Agency." American Experience. The Wild West, n.d. Accessed September 4, 2018. pbs.org/wgbh/americanexperience/features/ biography/james-agency/

Pinkerton staff. "Our History." Pinkerton, 2016. pinkerton.com/about-us/history/

Stone, AC, JE Starrs, and M. Stoneking. "Mitochondrial DNA Analysis of the Presumptive Remains of Jesse James." Department of Anthropology, Pennsylvania State University. PubMed, January 2001. 46(1). ncbi.nlm.nih.gov/pubmed/11210907

BILLY THE KID

Brothers, Marcelle. "Fact vs. Myth." About Billy the Kid, n.d. Last modified October 13, 2015. aboutbillythekid.com/fact_vs_myth.htm

Felony Guide Staff. "Is Grand Theft Auto a Felony?" FelonyGuide, 2016. felonyguide.com/ Is-grand-theft-auto-a-felony.php

"Inflation Calculator." Davemanuel.com, 2016. davemanuel.com/inflation-calculator.php

Klein, Christopher. "Historian Seeks Death Certificate to End Billy the Kid Rumors." History. A&E Networks, February 27, 2015. history.com/news/historian-seeks-death-certificate-to-end-billy-the-kid-rumors

Kopel, David. "Sheriffs and the Posse Comitatus." The Volokh Conspiracy. *The Washington Post,* May 15, 2014. washingtonpost.com/news/volokh-conspiracy/wp/2014/05/15/ sheriffs-and-the-posse-comitatus/?utm_term=.d85e1228ee1d

McClannahan, Rory. "Joining the U.S. Was No Simple Task for New Mexico." *Mountain View Telegraph,* January 5, 2012. mvtelegraph.com/news/joining-the-u-s-was-no-simple-task-for-new/article_c899dd97-2061-5a97-9f2c-bf915d5e5632.html

O'Toole, Fintan. "The Many Stories of Billy the Kid." The Annals of History. *The New Yorker.* Conde Nast, December 28, 1998. newyorker.com/magazine/1998/12/28/the-many-stories-of-billy-the-kid

Pounds, Ron. "Old Fort Sumner and 'Billy the Kid's' Grave." The Historical Marker
     Database, June 16, 2016. hmdb.org/Marker.asp?Marker=73713
"States by Order of Entry into the Union." Infoplease. Sandbox Networks, Inc., 2016.
     infoplease.com/ipa/A0763770.html

MATA HARI

Duffy, Michael. "Who's Who—Mata Hari." Firstworldwar.com, August 22, 2009.
     firstworldwar.com/bio/matahari.htm
Editors of Encyclopedia Britannica. "Mata Hari: Dutch Dancer and Spy." *Encyclopedia
     Britannica,* October 14, 2010. britannica.com/biography/Mata-Hari-Dutch-dancer-
     and-spy
"Femme fatale," et al. Merriam-Webster, 2017. merriam-webster.com/dictionary/
Howe, Russell Warren. "Mournful Fate of Mata Hari, The Spy Who Wasn't Guilty: New
     Evidence Indicates That the World War I Siren Was Executed Because Her Death Was
     Convenient to German and French Intelligence." *Smithsonian,* May 1986. trove.nla.gov.
     au/work/42110096?q&versionId=54988993
Mlong43. "Mata Hari." Spymuseum.com, March 18, 2015. spymuseum.com/mata-hari/

TYPHOID MARY

"Cholera—*Vibrio Cholerae* Infection." Centers for Disease Control and Prevention.
     November 6, 2014. cdc.gov/cholera/general/
"Dr. George Albert Soper, [Sr., II]." Brookhaven South Haven Hamlets & Their People,
     2011. brookhavensouthhaven.org/hamletpeople/tng/getpersonphp?personID=I14273&
     tree=hamlet
eastrivernyc.org. "Geography: The Islands: Randalls & Wards Island." East River NYC,
     2008. eastrivernyc.org/content/geography/the-islands/randalls-wards.html
Editors of Encyclopedia Britannica. "Bacteriology." *Encyclopedia Britannica,* September 7,
     2010. britannica.com/science/bacteriology
"Irish Crisis of 1879–80, The." Internet Archive, n.d. Accessed September 4, 2018. archive.
     org/stream/irishcrisisof18700dubluoft/irishcrisisof18700dubluoft_djvu.txt
libraryirelandcom. "Ireland's Loss of Population." Library Ireland, 2015. libraryireland.
     com/articles/LossPopulationOutlookIrelandDunraven/
Kennedy, Robert C. "On This Day." *The New York Times,* 2001. nytimes.com/learning/
     general/onthisday/harp/0228.html
Leavitt, Judith Walzer. "Typhoid Mary: Villain or Victim?" Nova. PBS, October 12, 2004.
     pbs.org/wgbh/nova/body/typhoid-mary-villain-or-victim.html
"Mary Alice Walker: Typhoid Mary." Marvel Universe Wiki. Marvel, 2017. marvel.com/
     universe/Typhoid_Mary
"WHO Guidelines on Hand Hygiene in Health Care: First Global Patient Safety Challenge
     Clean Care Is Safer Care." World Health Organization, 2009. ncbi.nlm.nih.gov/books/
     NBK144018/

RASPUTIN

"Alexei Romanov." In History/Russia, n.d. Accessed September 4, 2018. historyofrussia.
    org/alexei-romanov/
Azar, Helen. "The Romanov Family." The Romanov Family, 2015. theromanovfamily.com/
Biography.com Editors. "Anastasia Romanov Biography." Biography.com. A&E Television
    Networks, June 21, 2016. biography.com/people/anastasia-9184008#mystery
Daniels, Robert V. "The Mad Monk." *The New York Times,* June 11, 2000. nytimes.com/
    books/00/06/11/reviews/000611.11dani.html
Fyfe, Duncan. "The Strange Reason Nearly Every Film Ends by Saying It's Fiction
    (You Guessed It: Rasputin!)." Browbeat. Slate, August 26, 2016. slate.com/blogs/
    browbeat/2016/08/26/the_bizarre_true_story_behind_the_this_is_a_work_of_fiction_
    disclaimer.html

VINCENZO PERUGGIA

"Art & Antiques." Metropolitan Police, 2017. content.met.police.uk/Site/artandantiques
Brooks, Peter. "Napoleon's Eye." *The New York Review of Books.* November 19, 2009,
    nybooks.com/articles/2009/11/19/napoleons-eye/
Caesar, Ed. "What Is the Value of Stolen Art?" *The New York Times Magazine.* November
    13, 2013. nytimes.com/2013/11/17/magazine/what-is-the-value-of-stolen-art.html?_
    r=0
FBI Staff. "The Gardner Museum Theft: Reward Offered for Return of Artwork." FBI. U.S.
    Department of Justice, March 18, 2013. fbi.gov/news/stories/5-million-reward-offered-
    for-return-of-stolen-gardner-museum-artwork
FBI Staff. "Historic Footage Connected to Gardner Museum Burglary Released, Public
    Assistance Sought." FBI Boston Division. U.S. Department of Justice, August 6,
    2015. fbi.gov/contact-us/field-offices/boston/news/press-releases/historic-footage-
    connected-to-gardner-museum-burglary-released-public-assistance-sought
"Technologies." Visible Proofs: Forensic Views of the Body. U.S. National Library of
    Medicine, February 16, 2006. nlm.nih.gov/visibleproofs/galleries/technologies/
    bertillon_image_3.html
"What We Investigate." Federal Bureau of Investigation Art Crime Team. FBI, n.d.
    Accessed September 4, 2018. fbi.gov/investigate/violent-crime/art-theft

BERNARD OTTO KUEHN

"About Us." German American Internee Coalition, n.d. gaic.info
Cohen, Andrew. "Treatment of Japanese-Americans in WWII Hawaii Revealed in
    Article." UC Berkeley School of Law, May 5, 2011. law.berkeley.edu/article/treatment-
    of-japanese-americans-in-wwii-hawaii-revealed-in-article/
Deac, Wil. "Takeo Yoshikawa: World War II Japanese Pearl Harbor Spy." HistoryNet, June
    12, 2006. historynet.com/takeo-yoshikawa-world-war-ii-japanese-pearl-harbor-spy.htm

FBI Staff. "Bernard Kuehn, Part 1 of 7, File Number 65-1574." FBI Records: The Vault. 2016. vault.fbi.gov/bernard-julius-otto-kuehn/bernard-julius-otto-kuehn/view

FBI. "A Byte Out of History, Sheets, Sails, and Dormer Lights: The Case of the Pearl Harbor Spy." FBI, February 21, 2005. archives.fbi.gov/archives/news/stories/2005/february/kuehn_022105

FBI. "FBI Honolulu History." Field Office Histories. FBI, 2016. fbi.gov/history/field-office-histories/honolulu

FBI Staff. "Sheets, Sails, and Dormer Lights: The Case of the Pearl Harbor Spy." In A Byte Out of History. FBI, February 21, 2005. archives.fbi.gov/archives/news/stories/2005/february/kuehn_022105

"Germans at Pearl Harbor." Germany Watch. December 8, 2012. germanywatch.blogspot.com/2012/12/germans-at-pearl-harbor.html

Hirayama, Laura. "Repercussions of the 'Day of Infamy': From the Smoke of Pearl." *The Hawaii Herald,* vol. 2, no. 23, December 4, 1981. nisei.hawaii.edu/object/io_1149133013500.html

"Kamikaze." United States History, n.d. Accessed September 4, 2018. u-s-history.com/pages/h1740.html

"Nazi." Online Etymology Dictionary, 2017. etymonline.com/index.php?term=Nazi

Nix, Elizabeth. "6 People You Didn't Know Were WWII Spies." History. A&E Networks, November 11, 2014. history.com/news/history-lists/6-people-you-didnt-know-were-wwii-spies

Onion, Rebecca. "Some Choice Bits of Slang from American Soldiers Serving in WWII." The Vault. Slate, November 11, 2013. slate.com/blogs/the_vault/2013/11/11/military_slang_terms_used_by_soldiers_in_wwii.html

"Proceedings of Army Pearl Harbor Board." Ibiblio. University of North Carolina at Chapel Hill, n.d. Accessed September 4, 2018. ibiblio.org/pha/congress/Army%20Board%20Exhibits/Exhibit%2052.pdf

"Remembering Pearl Harbor: A Pearl Harbor Fact Sheet." US Census Bureau. National WWII Museum, n.d. Accessed September 4, 2018. census.gov/history/pdf/pearl-harbor-fact-sheet-1.pdf

Young, Peter T. "Postcards, Sails, Sheets, Lights, Ads, Fires, and Radio Signals." LinkedIn, December 7, 2014. linkedin.com/pulse/20141207171952-88723353-postcards-sails-sheets-lights-ads-fires-and-radio-signals

ANNA ANDERSON

Andrews, Evan. "7 People Who Pretended to be Royals." History. A&E Networks, May 21, 2013. history.com/news/history-lists/7-people-who-pretended-to-be-royals

Bailey, Penny. "Before DNA: 20th-Century Forensics." Phys.org, September 6, 2011. phys.org/news/2011-09-dna-20th-century-forensics.html

Calandro, Lisa, et al. "Evolution of DNA Evidence for Crime Solving: A Judicial and Legislative History. *Forensic Magazine.* Advantage Business Media, January 6, 2005. forensicmag.com/article/2005/01/evolution-dna-evidence-crime-solving-judicial-and-legislative-history

"Facts and History of Graphology." Handwriting Research Corporation, 2016. handwriting.com/facts/history.html

Hirby, J. "History of DNA Testing in Criminal Cases." The Law Dictionary, n.d. Accessed September 4, 2018. thelawdictionary.org/article/history-of-dna-testing-in-criminal-cases/

Legacy Staff. "Anna Anderson: The Great Imposter." Explore History. Legacy.com, 2016. legacy.com/news/explore-history/article/anna-anderson-the-great-imposter

Knyaz, Velikye. "The Imperial Children's Remains Discovered FAQs. Please Read!" Discussion Forum. The Alexander Palace Time Machine, 2015. forum.alexanderpalace. org/index.php?topic=10115.msg282450#msg282450

Moffeit, Miles, and Susan Greene. "Room for Error in the Evidence Vaults." *The Denver Post,* July 22, 2007. denverpost.com/2007/07/22/room-for-error-in-evidence-vaults/

"Sarbah vs. Home Office, Ghana Immigration Case, 1985." DNA Fingerprinting, n.d. Accessed September 4, 2018. dnafingerprinting19.tripod.com/id14.html

Spohn, Julie A. "The Legal Implications of Graphology." *Washington University Law Review,* vol. 75, issue 3, January 1997. openscholarship.wustl.edu/cgi/viewcontent. cgi?article=1584&context=law_lawreview

"Tracking People—Checklist." History Detectives: Special Investigations. PBS, 2014. pbs. org/opb/historydetectives/technique/tracking-people-checklist/

Tucker, William O. Jr. "Jack & Anna: Remembering the Czar of Charlottesville Eccentrics." The Hook. Better Publications, LLC, July 5, 2007. readthehook. com/86004/cover-jack-amp-anna-remembering-czar-charlottesville-eccentrics

Wagner, Stephen. "True Stories of Doppelgangers." About Entertainment. ThoughtCo., April 10, 2016. paranormal.about.com/od/Doppelgangers/a/doppelgangers.htm

AL CAPONE

Crime Museum. "Ballistics." Crime Museum, LLC, 2016. crimemuseum.org/crime-library/ballistics/

Dowd, Katie. "Historic Photos of Alcatraz Prison." SFGATE.com. Hearst Communications, 2016. sfgate.com/bayarea/slideshow/40th-anniversary-of-Alcatraz-opening-to-the-public-72463/photo-4342802.php

Eig, Jonathan. "The St. Valentine's Day Massacre and Al Capone—Excerpt from *Get Capone.*" *Chicago Magazine,* April 30, 2010. chicagomag.com/Chicago-Magazine/May-2010/Get-Capone-St-Valentines-Day-Massacre-Jonathan-Eig/

FBI Staff. "FBI's Ten Most Wanted Fugitives: 60th Anniversary." Federal Bureau of Investigation. U.S. Department of Justice, 2010. fbi.gov/stats-services/publications/ten-most-wanted-fugitives-60th-anniversary-1950-2010.pdf

FBI. "Solving Scarface: How the Law Finally Caught Up with Al Capone." Federal Bureau of Investigation. U.S. Department of Justice, March 28, 2005. archives.fbi.gov/archives/news/stories/2005/march/capone_032805

History Channel. "Prohibition." History.com. A&E Networks, 2009. history.com/topics/prohibition

Military Factory. "American War Deaths Throughout History." Militaryfactory.com, 2016.

militaryfactory.com/american_war_deaths.asp

National Archives. "World War I Draft Registration Cards." National Archives. U.S. National Archives and Records Administration, 2016. archives.gov/research/military/ww1/draft-registration

Nix, Elizabeth. "6 Infamous Imposters." History. A&E Networks, August 19, 2014. history.com/news/history-lists/6-infamous-impostors

O'Brien, John. "The St. Valentine's Day Massacre." *Chicago Tribune,* February 14, 2014. chicagotribune.com/news/nationworld/politics/chi-chicagodays-valentinesmassacre-story-story.html

Oregon Public Broadcasting. "Ballistics." History Detectives: Special Investigations. PBS, 2014. pbs.org/opb/historydetectives/technique/ballistics/

Rose, I. Nelson. "Gambling and the Law: Pivotal Dates." Frontline. PBS.org, 1997. pbs.org/wgbh/pages/frontline/shows/gamble/etc/cron.html

"Sharon V. Hill." Law.gov. Publish.Resource.org, 2016. law.resource.org/pub/us/case/reporter/F/0024/0024.f.0726.pdf

Willbanks, James H. "Machine Guns: An Illustrated History of Their Impact." ABC-CLIO, 2004. books.google.co.uk/books?id=VWkYoAkoMHIC&pg=PA87&lpg=PA87&dq=chicago+piano+thompson&source=bl&ots=HFsYkShru8&sig=GVc3ez3dDi8_PjRlk-Fir1NDn10&hl=en&sa=X&ei=8Vl4U_74FsftPIeZgLgK#v=onepage&q=chicago%20piano%20thompson&f=false

INDEX

at Sloane Hospital for Women, 117, 122
typhus, 121

Uffizi Gallery, 144
United States Express Company, 79–80
United States v. Alphonse Capone, 187
U.S. Supreme Court, 187

Venezuela, 146
Virginia, 24–25, 51, 55, 61, 64–68, 167, 173
von Rathlef-Kleilmann, Harriet, 171

Waite, Charles, 193
War Department, 65, 153, 162
Warne, Kate, 84
Washington, D.C., 62–65, 68, 164
Wendell, Andrew, 72
Wild West, 89–90
  slang of, 96
witchcraft, 1–2, 13–14, 16
Witness Protection Program, 187, 192
World War I, 99, 103, 108, 129, 153, 182
World War II, 153, 159–160
  slang of, 165
Wright, Wilbur, 120

Yusupov, Felix, 129–132, 134, 136
Yusupov, Irina, 129–130, 136

Zelle, Margaretha, *see* Mata Hari